MORE
FROM THE QUARRIES
OF
LAST CHANCE GULCH
VOLUME III

JON AXLINE
ELLEN BAUMLER
DAVID COLE
CHERE JIUSTO
MARTHA KOHL
LEANNE KURTZ
HARRIETT C. MELOY
VIVIAN A. PALADIN
SARA SCOTT
DAVE SHORS
STEPHENIE AMBROSE TUBBS
DAVE WALTER
MARCELLA WALTER

Doris Rush, Publisher

Softbound ISBN 1-56037-130-7
Hardbound ISBN 1-56037-133-1

Prepared for publication by
Montana Magazine

Printed in Canada

CONTENTS

Introduction

After a lifetime of watching journalists weave the fabric of a story from developing and often incomplete details, it's especially satisfying to be involved with the historians who research and write "More From the Quarries of Last Chance Gulch" for the *Independent Record*, first in the popular weekly newspaper column, then in this book form.

The tools of a historian—the letters, notes, cards, oral recollections, photographs, books and newspaper articles—don't seem much different than those of a journalist. But the mere element of passing time puts them into a different arena, one of conclusion.

The bits and pieces of history might be neatly catalogued in the Montana Historical Society Library, or they might be found in a cardboard box in someone's basement. Our "Quarries" authors know and explore all the obvious sources, plus they are experts at extracting facts from the side gulches of Helena's past.

Without these efforts, much of what brought us to this place in time could become footnotes or less in our recorded history. The Quarries authors have been committed to this fulfillment from the beginning of the weekly newspaper column in March 1994, and the publication of the first volume of this book.

I can vividly remember that day in November 1995 when Volume I of *More From the Quarries of Last Chance Gulch* was just back from the printer. Sitting around the large table in the *Independent Record*'s second-floor conference room were members of the original group: Jon Axline, Ellen Baumler, Chere Jiusto, Leanne Kurtz, Harriett C. Meloy, Richard B. Roeder, Dave Walter and me. All the writers signed the limited edition leather bound copies. Everyone felt a sincere sense of satisfaction that these Helena stories were now neatly saved in a book for other generations.

The weekly Quarries newspaper column had quickly become a favorite regular feature in the *Independent Record*.

Now the book was to take its place as one of Helena's most popular bound volumes. Rich Roeder was fascinated, and somewhat puzzled by the whole process. As a professional historian, professor and author of note, he wasn't quite sure if he should be associated with a newspaper, where that first rough draft of history was being written on a daily basis. But he loved Helena's history, he loved the group of Quarries writers and the comradeship they had established. The first book somewhat cemented the relationship. But he remained amazed by the popularity of the column. I vividly remember a story he told us that day. He was walking out of the Cathedral of St. Helena after Sunday mass, he said. A friend stopped him and introduced Rich to the man's wife. "Sure," the wife replied upon hearing Roeder's name. "You write that history column in the paper." It seems the man who had co-authored the definitive Montana history book *Montana: A History of Two Centuries* had discovered a new audience as a Quarries author.

Rich Roeder died two days before Christmas in 1995. The second *Quarries* book, published in 1996, was dedicated to his memory.

That second volume included the work of two new Quarries regulars, Kimberly Morrison and Vivian A. Paladin. Two of Richard Roeder's last written works were in this volume. Also, the book ended with a comprehensive section about Helena's earthquakes of 1935 and 1936.

With the second book, Quarries seemed to have more credibility: Two volumes in print, with seventy-six stories about notable Helena places, events and people. The books were welcomed into Helena's libraries and schools where they quickly became dog-eared as often-used sources for term papers and research projects.

Plus, with publication of the second volume there was a parallel in history, where all things meld. The column and books originally were named in honor of the two published books of lifelong Helena newspaperman William C. Campbell, called *From the Quarries of Last Chance Gulch: A "News-History" of Helena*. Campbell's books represented the first concerted attempt to tell the story of the Helena community. Campbell's book covers were blue and red, as were the covers of our first two Quarries volumes.

History is a blending of great and small, and often of failures that lead to success. One of the original Quarries authors, Jon Axline, writes in this volume about the trials of John B. Wilson: "I Would Like to Quit the Mountains." Wilson's life was like that of many adventurers who came to Helena in the 1860s to search for placer riches. If it wasn't for Axline's Quarries story about his life, you'd never know his name. Yet, your understanding of Helena's history is much richer after you read this account. With Wilson's placer operation near Blackfoot City failing in the late 1870s, he wrote in utter frustration: "My life is entirely misspent but alas! It is too late to rectify it now."

But salvation arrived in the form of two men who bought his mine. With $8,000 in his pocket, Wilson found new opportunities in real estate and farming.

At the time of his death in April, 1912, "The 84-year-old was remembered as a 'man who was not only a pioneer of Montana, but one who by the force of his makeup and character, as well as by his blameless life, attained a high position of esteem and regard of his fellow men'." Students of history learn to be patient.

Ellen Baumler's captivating tale about "The Lady of the House: Grandstreet Theatre's Ghost" recognizes that not all history is measured by tangible influences.

"Footsteps that echo in an empty building," Baumler writes in her lyrical style. "A name softly whispered when no one else is there, the feeling that someone is watching from the shadows, a fleeting rush of cold air and other unexplained occurrences like these are not so unusual at Grandstreet Theatre."

Baumler's story is of Clara Bicknell Hodgin, "whose legacy evidently reaches far beyond her all-too-brief time in Helena." After her death in 1905 at the age of thirty-four, friends established a memorial fund and collected $500 that was used to commission a beautiful stained glass window by Louis Comfort Tiffany. The window, which was installed in Helena's Unitarian Church, was later placed in storage when the building became the city library in 1933. It wasn't until 1976 that it was discovered in the Civic Center basement. It was reinstalled that year in the old church building, which had become the home for a new community theatre, the Grandstreet.

It seems that Clara Hodgin's spirit was firmly installed with the beautiful Tiffany.

"There is no question in the minds of most of the folks at the Grandstreet that there is some extraordinary energy at work in the place," Baumler writes. They are "convinced that the energy, or spirit, is Clara," she continues.

The Quarries writers also have extraordinary energy, and an intense curiosity about some of the little remembered and unusual members of the community—the underdogs of history—who have made contributions to Helena's distinctive character.

They can't ignore the obvious, though, the men, women and places that immediately bring Helena to mind.

One case in point is Harriett C. Meloy's story about Charles A. Broadwater, leader of men, director of opinion, whose name is most readily associated with his splendid resort and natatorium that was located just west of Helena.

"Broadwater's first career began when he purchased a wagon, bought cattle from farmers in the Deer Lodge Valley, and hauled beef to the mines," Meloy writes. Later he hauled materials up the Missouri from St. Louis and operated both Fort Assinniboine and Fort Maginnis at different times. But his eyes turned to Helena, where he made a fortune in banking and real estate.

His proudest moment must have been when the beautiful Broadwater Hotel was dedicated in August 1889. "Broadwater's natatorium was designed to be the largest and most splendid of its kind in the world," Meloy writes. "When construction of the hotel and natatorium was completed it was estimated that a full half million dollars was expended."

For Dave Walter, a consummate researcher, nothing quite piques his interest like a good mystery. In this volume he tells us, "Indeed, not all of Helena's crimes have been solved or the criminals punished. Even when evidence abounds and authorities develop several prime suspects, sometimes justice is not served."

Just such a case was the 1909 murder of forty-year-old John Hancock, who arrived in Montana with his parents in 1877, at the front door of St. John's Hospital on Catholic Hill. The *Montana Daily Record* called the deed "...one of the most shocking, premeditated, cold-blooded, and dastardly assaults ever attempted in Lewis and Clark County."

In his account, Walter takes the reader back and investigates this most dastardly crime. And by the end of his column, most readers must wonder why this murder remains one of Helena's prime "unsolved mysteries."

Leanne Kurtz reminds us that famed artist R.E. DeCamp initially disliked Helena, but later the good friend of Charles M. Russell found his most captivating subjects in this area.

"DeCamp was particularly enthralled with the Gates of the Mountains," writes Kurtz, "and spent considerable time at Nicolas Hilger's ranch on the Missouri—sketching, painting, and wooing one of Hilger's young daughters."

If you let your imagination flow and listen carefully, DeCamp's rippling rivers can still be heard in Montana's capitol. His four feet by eight feet panels in room 312-2 in the capitol serve as a tour of Montana through DeCamp's eyes.

Also contributing to this third Quarries volume are Vivian Paladin, Chere Jiusto, Stephenie Ambrose Tubbs, Sara Scott, Marcella Walter, Martha Kohl and David Cole.

Helenans owe much to this cadre of writers who are so fascinated with the history of our place; they spend countless hours and days researching these stories.

The community, and these writers are also grateful to the people at the *Independent Record* who have supported this project. They include former publisher Bruce Whittenberg, who immediately recognized the importance of this column for the paper; present publisher Doris Rush for her continuing support; Editor Charles Wood; IR Business Manager Jolene Selby; and other members of the IR management team.

We'd also like to thank the staff at the Montana Historical Society for their help in locating research materials, especially Lory Morrow, Becca Kohl, and Bonnie Morgan of the Society's photo archives.

It's amazing how much of our history is not passed down

from generation to generation, and is lost with the people who hold those memories. But as we approach the new millenium, we can feel confident that Helena's roots are firmly reflected in these three Quarries books, and from these roots will spring forth the fascinating new life of the 21st century. We can't begin to imagine what that will be. But, to those who build their lives here, we hope to convey our respect and love for this place and its people.

Dave Shors
Associate Editor, Independent Record

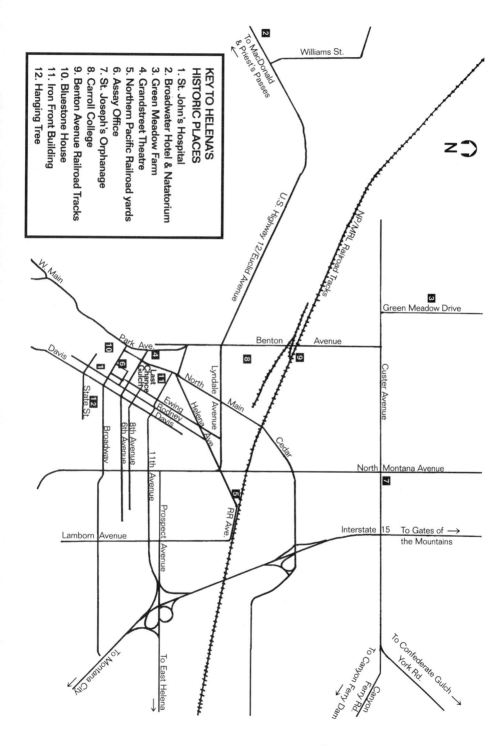

KEY TO HELENA'S
HISTORIC PLACES

1. St. John's Hospital
2. Broadwater Hotel & Natatorium
3. Green Meadow Farm
4. Grandstreet Theatre
5. Northern Pacific Railroad yards
6. Assay Office
7. St. Joseph's Orphanage
8. Carroll College
9. Benton Avenue Railroad Tracks
10. Bluestone House
11. Iron Front Building
12. Hanging Tree

PEOPLE

Ancient Artists of Central Montana

By Sara Scott

Prehistoric paintings in rockshelters, caves, and rock over-hangs fascinate modern people. Today, images drawn by Indians centuries ago are reproduced on countless T-shirts, posters, and coffee mugs. Thousands of people view the "Indian paintings" within the Gates of the Mountains each year and hundreds visit the Hellgate Canyon paintings in the nearby Big Belt Mountains. Though ancient American Indian rock art is deeply intriguing, the meaning these paintings express is little known, and fanciful but often inaccurate interpretations abound.

The science of archaeology attempts to render a systematic interpretation of these paintings. With an emphasis on the works' age, function, and distribution across the landscape, archaeologists work to decipher the patterns and meaning reflected by these paintings.

For the uninitiated, what is this ancient art? Archaeologists refer to the paintings and carvings left on rock surfaces

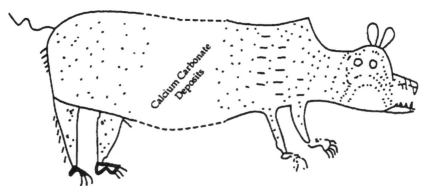

Sketch of a grizzly bear found in Rainbow Bear Cave.

by American Indians as "rock art." The paintings are called "pictographs," whereas etched or carved images are referred to as "petroglyphs."

Archaeological surveys across Montana show that over 680 sites reflect the artistic talents of Montana's ancient peoples. In central Montana, these sites appear in relatively isolated areas, often at the mouths and heads of small canyons. Typically, they are painted or carved in shallow rockshelters or under slight rock overhangs not far from streams. Rock art also appears in caverns where artificial light is needed to view figures painted in places of eternal and complete darkness.

Rock art designs vary by region. The Northwestern Plains designs are quite different from those found farther west on the Columbia Plateau. In the late 1970s, Forest Service archaeologist Dr. James Keyser classified the rock art of central Montana as the "Central Montana Abstract Style" because of the abstract human, animal, and geometric designs that grace the limestone canyons and rock faces here. Over 150 rock art sites recorded north of Helena exhibit handprints, fingerlines, and paint smears, some of which are over 1,500 years old. The fingerlines are not the short, neat tally marks or "day counts" found in the pictographs of western Montana but rather are long streaks made with the central three fingers. Handprints occur in groups of five to fifteen and consist of solid hand impressions made by dipping the palm-side of the hand in paint, then pressing the hand against the rock. Hand outlines were also drawn. Northeast of Helena in the Smith River drainage, archaeologists Drs. Mavis and John Greer of Casper, Wyoming, found the majority of hand impressions and outlines are of the right hand, with only one third being made with the left hand. In some cases, they could identify the gender of the painter because men have a longer ring finger than they do index finger whereas for females the opposite is true.

In central Montana, figures of humans appear in a variety of forms with attached headdresses, horns, upraised arms, no arms, or wing-like arms. Some figures lack hands, feet, or heads while others display physical features denoting gender. Throughout Montana and much of the world, ancient rock art typically depicts humans with bows, arrows, spears, and atlatls (spear throwers) engaged in hunting, but these scenes are absent in central Montana. Both the Greers and Keyser believe that some of the human figures are associated with the activities of American Indian shamans. Shamans were people considered as healers among their tribes. Because they possessed supernatural power, shamans were sometimes feared. Archaeologists ascribe shamanistic qualities to these central Montana rock art figures because they are found in secluded or semi-secluded areas in contrast to the hard-to-access western Montana paintings associated with vision questing and puberty rites, or the massive paintings that call for public attention located along the Sun River near Great Falls. The presence of horns and headdresses and the lack of certain body parts are also well documented indications of shamanistic power. Large body shields, though often associated with warfare, were sometimes painted by shamans to provide protection from the supernatural rather than from earthly warfare. Figures of shamans were sometimes painted on the edge of a crack in the rock, possibly denoting passage from or into another world or spiritual domain.

Animal pictographs are not common in this part of the state, but otters, bears, lizards, bison, elk, birds, and rabbits occasionally appear in rock art. Interestingly, the animals that occur most often, such as the bear and turtle, are not food staples but instead are associated with the supernatural, ceremonies, and rituals. Turtle figures are prolific along the Smith River and their co-occurrence with shaman figures suggests they held supernatural power, as they did in other parts of North America. Bear figures and tracks are especially prominent in central Montana rock art and are portrayed as complete animal, head only, or just paws or tracks. All identified bears are grizzlies, as reflected by long claws and the characteristic humps on their backs. Bear designs are not associated with hunting or killing because no weapons or other indicators of death appear in the rock art panels. Bear imagery first appeared in Montana about 2,000 years ago as anatomically correct designs showing front and back outlined paws. An especially intriguing bear pictograph is found at Bear Mask Cave. Here a bear face is painted around the entrance to the cave so

Hand impressions found near the Smith River.

that one literally walks into the cave through the mouth of a giant bear. Imagine a shaman chanting from inside the cave at night so that it appeared as if the bear actually produced the sounds. It is no wonder shamans were treated reverently, if not feared.

Keyser originally proposed that the Central Montana Abstract style rock art functioned as a part of rituals and ceremonies associated with shamanistic activities. But Mavis Greer, who researched Smith River rock art as part of her doctoral dissertation, found that only one third of the sites she studied were associated with the practices of shamans. Instead, she believes that rock art at some sites served as a marker, similar to a modern-day billboard, announcing messages for all to see. Hand prints, animal tracks, and clan symbols (either animal or geometric) served to identify a prehistoric group and perhaps define its territory. She and Keyser agree that many Smith River rock art panels were painted to record an event of an individual or a tribe. This "biographical" rock art style includes shield figures, hunted animals, trails, hoof prints, and tipis. This style became common between 1750 and 1900 when a rapid shift in warfare and status acquisition occurred as a result of the introduction of the horse and gun from Euro-American explorers and traders. During this time, rock art changed dramatically from shamanistic or clan abstractions to very realistic scenes showing detailed movement and the passage of time. Scenes of warfare, horse stealing, dancing, coup counting and hunting were exquisitely drawn during this period of major cultural change. This rock art style was duplicated on painted buffalo robes and in ledger book drawings of American Indians, and it enables archaeologists like Jim Keyser to decipher the meaning of many biographical rock art designs.

Pictographs were painted with liquid paint and crayons.

Crayons consisted of lumps of raw pigment or Indian-made "greasepaint" markers. Paint was derived mostly from charcoal or locally obtained hematite which occurs in a variety of colors. The most common paint colors are various hues of red and orange, black, and yellow. Valuable paint pigment sources, such as one reported in a cave in the Big Belt Mountains, were extensively excavated using antler digging tools. These pigment sources were coveted by Montana Indian groups, such as the Salish, who continued to use them up until historic times. Native people mixed their paints with binding agents that included water, plant juice, urine, blood, and animal fat. Pictographs were fashioned with fingers, hands, brushes, and crayons. Although rock art conjures images of ancient hair-bristle brushes, of the 1,687 rock art figures analyzed by Mavis Greer, 1,122 were applied with fingers, 294 with hands, 165 with crayons, and only eight with brushes. The application method of the remaining figures could not be deciphered. Most pictographs are monochrome (one color) but bichrome (two colors) paintings occasionally occur; polychrome (more than two colors) paintings are practically absent in Montana.

The age of prehistoric rock art can be dated by various means including radiocarbon dating (taken from the organic binders in paint), superimpositioning, figure content cross dating, and seriation. The most commonly used method is superimpositioning where later paintings occur on top of earlier designs. Radiocarbon dating is the most absolute method of dating but is only successful when organic compounds were used as paint binders. In central Montana, Indian people painted pictures as early as 2,000 years ago and continued this artistic practice into the historic period.

Despite the fact that rock art sites have survived the forces of nature for many hundreds of years, most of these sites are extremely fragile, and many are considered sacred by contemporary Indian people. Direct contact with pictographs and petroglyphs can damage their aesthetic, scientific, and spiritual value. Viewers should take care to not touch rock art surfaces or make rubbings or casts without professional assistance. To capture the fascinating beauty of this ancient art, black and white or color photographs provide the best means.

ANCIENT STONE WORKERS OF THE HELENA VALLEY

✤

BY SARA SCOTT

The striking of hammerstones against chert cobbles was a familiar sound in the forested draws near present-day Montana City some 9,300 years ago. "Paleoindian" cultures of long ago frequented this area of the Helena Valley in search of quality toolstone for the manufacture of stone projectile points, knives, and scrapers so essential to their survival. These and later Indian peoples dug into the earth with antler and wood digging sticks in search of chert nodules and boulders suitable for flintknapping, creating subtle depressions that today can easily be mistaken for shallow miners' prospect pits. As stone was exposed, the raw cobbles were tested by knocking off sample flakes. Decent material was then pared down by further "percussion flaking" in which a fist-sized hammerstone or antler baton was used to knock off extraneous material, creating large, leaf-shaped artifacts that archaeologists call "bifaces." Many of these bifaces were broken during manufacture and discarded, likely resulting in much prehistoric cussing. The stone bifaces were then easily transported in skin bags back to campsites where they provided the raw toolstock for months to come. Stone flakes struck off these biface cores, and many of the bifaces themselves, were manufactured into an array of utilitarian implements, including exquisitely made projectile points.

This reconstruction of early Paleoindian prehistoric stone quarrying and tool manufacture in the Helena Valley is based on archaeological evidence from the well-known MacHaffie archaeological site which is listed in the National Register of

Historic Places. The site is located on private property along a spring-fed perennial stream less than six miles southeast of Helena. First excavated in 1951 by Dr. Richard Forbis and other archaeologists from Columbia and Montana State universities, the site yielded some of the first evidence of ancient "Cody Complex" and "Folsom" prehistoric occupations in Montana. But many questions were left unanswered about the site and its inhabitants.

Starting in 1989, a team of geologists and archaeologists led by Dr. Leslie Davis of the Museum of the Rockies, Montana State University-Bozeman (MSU), began reexamining the MacHaffie site to obtain paleoecological data about the early environment of the area and to better understand the sequence of prehistoric occupations there. To date, Davis' team has obtained numerous radiocarbon dates from the site, which place its most ancient occupants there between 9,340 and 8,280 years ago. The investigators learned that the Folsom (dated to 9,340 years ago), and slightly later Cody Complex (dated to between 8,620 and 8,280 years ago) groups made plentiful use of the locally quarried Montana City chert to make their distinctive and delicately flaked Folsom and "Scottsbluff" (Cody Complex) projectile points and tools. The recovery of bison, deer, wolf, and rabbit remains is testimony to the hearty meals of Folsom peoples. Although the more recent habitations, denoted by arrow points dating back to 1500 years ago, are only a peripheral focus of the MSU-Bozeman investigations, their presence demonstrates that, for over a period of approximately 8,000 years, people kept coming back to this site to quarry stone, make tools, hunt animals, and camp.

The early Paleoindian cultures of the American West have fascinated archaeologists since 1927 when the remains of twenty-three extinct bison (*Bison antiquus*) were discovered in a box canyon in undisputed association with nineteen Folsom projectile points. The "Folsom culture" and its characteristic Folsom point in particular, capture the archaeological imagination. Folsom projectile points are distinctive because they have a long, channel flake or "flute" removed from the base of the point on both sides of the artifact—a flintknapping technique that is difficult to execute.

Many modern-day flint-knappers attempt to replicate Folsom points in order to learn how they were manufactured. In replicating Folsom points from the Lindenmeier site in Colorado, expert flintknapper Dr. Jeff Flenniken, of Pullman, Washington, found that the characteristic channel flake is removed toward the end of the point-making process after many minutes are expended at careful pressure flaking with an antler tool. Flenniken also discovered that it

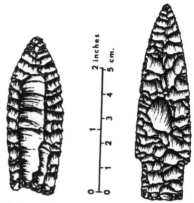

Left: Folsom projectile point showing the distinctive flute down the center of the point. Right: Scottsbluff projectile point.

took forty minutes to make one point. Further, during the fluting process, the breakage rate was about 37 percent, meaning that every third swing of the antler baton flirted with disaster. Based on his experimental studies, Flenniken believes that two people were required to produce the characteristic Folsom "flute": one to hold and position the Folsom pre-form and the other to apply the required force to drive off the channel flake from the artifact. Other experts argue that the flute can be removed by a single flintknapper with an antler baton or a hammerstone.

Whatever the case, the unique Folsom technology promises to perplex archaeologists for some time. Why the central flute? The most common explanation is that it facilitated attaching or "hafting" the projectile point onto a wooden shaft. Whether these points were propelled by a lance or an atlatl or throwing board is another question hotly debated by archaeologists. To date, the MSU-Bozeman researchers at MacHaffie have found neither complete nor broken Folsom points and, unfortunately, the artifacts from the 1951 excavations are missing. When such material is eventually found at MacHaffie, careful study of manufacturing techniques will be undertaken.

Research today into early Paleoindian sites goes well beyond the traditional focus on chipped stone projectile points and tools. The MSU-Bozeman team studying the MacHaffie site is highly interested in the environment of the area at the time of the prehistoric Folsom and Scottsbluff occupations. Analyses of pollen samples indicate that sagebrush steppe was dominant in this area throughout the last 10,000 years and that the valley floor was covered with riparian vegetation prior to 8,280 years ago. After this time, a marked increase in sagebrush pollen reflects a period of warmer and drier temperatures. Animal bone remains from a large canine (dog or wolf), and the forelimb and hindlimb bones of at least one bison, were also identified. Of importance, the size of the MacHaffie bison bones compares closely with extinct forms of bison *(Bison antiquus)* discovered at the Horner archaeological site in Wyoming. The types of bone left at MacHaffie indicate the use of selected carcass parts, while cut marks and impact scars from hammerstones reflect butchering and the removal of bone marrow.

Both Folsom and Cody Complex sites are very rare in Montana. In fact, most identified Folsom projectile points are surface finds with no other associated artifacts. This lack of Folsom-age sites may be due, in part, to the extensive hydraulic mining and development of river and creek terraces throughout the Helena Valley and adjacent Big Belt and Elkhorn mountains. In contrast, the number of Folsom points found in western North Dakota alone is double that of known surface and buried Folsom finds in Montana. Thus, imagine the excitement over the discovery of a Folsom-age site in 1982 in the Limestone Hills near Townsend, some twenty miles southeast of MacHaffie. This site, called Indian Creek, was also excavated by Dr. Leslie Davis of MSU-Bozeman in the mid-1980s. Here, a deeply buried site was found with Folsom-age artifacts including a distinct channel or flute flake. Folsom-age prehistoric groups camped at Indian Creek, based on radiocarbon dating, between 10,980 and 10,630 years ago. The 10,980 date is somewhat early for Folsom sites in the West since most date to between 10,900 and 10,200 years in age. Significantly, the Folsom occupation at MacHaffie dates much later in time (to 9,340 years ago). Although the discrepancy in dates between the two sites will be further studied, it now appears that the late dates from MacHaffie make its Folsom inhabitants some of the last people to use this ancient technology. Dr. Davis quips that, together, Indian Creek and MacHaffie make the Helena area both the "First and Last Best Place" for Folsom peoples.

Not surprisingly, the extent and nature of the information derived from the recent investigations at the MacHaffie site far surpass what was learned in the 1950s. This simple fact emphasizes the importance of conserving and protecting archaeological sites for future scientific study and analysis. In this technological age, it is mystifying to think of the information that might be realized by future archaeologists working at MacHaffie, Indian Creek, and other Paleoindian sites in the year 2050 and beyond. Without doubt, the MacHaffie site offers us a rare window into the past in which to visualize and learn about the activities and daily lives of ancient people. We now know that ancient residents of the Helena Valley returned year after year to MacHaffie to quarry stone, make exquisite hunting tools, and camp along a spring-fed perennial stream. Whom they traded with, where they hunted, how they were organized as groups, and how labor was divided between men and women are questions left to be resolved by future generations of Montana archaeologists.

THE DEPORTATION OF MAJOR JOHN OWEN

୧ୄ୶

BY ELLEN BAUMLER

Just outside Stevensville in the heart of the Bitterroot is a roadside stop, now a state monument, where an unhurried traveler can explore one of Montana's treasures. The partially-reconstructed buildings of Fort Owen chronicle an important chapter in our state's history and tell a story about a man whose presence there made a difference to many.

John Owen bought the mills, fields and buildings of St. Mary's Mission from the Jesuit priests who had established it in 1841. Owen relocated a short distance to the north and built a trading post within a log palisade. Appointed special agent to the Flathead Indians in 1856, Owen championed causes and tried to reason with the government on the Indians' behalf. His efforts continued even after his bitter resignation in 1862. Owen's widely renowned hospitality also buoyed weary trappers and travelers passing through his true oasis in the wilderness. The delicacies and fine spirits—even iced lemonade—offered guests at Fort Owen never failed to amaze his visitors. Lt. John Mullan speaks with astonishment of Owen's library, saying it was the finest in the northwest.

There were profound changes during the two decades from 1850 to 1870, from the westward movement on the Oregon Trail to the building of the Mullan Road (which bypassed Fort Owen), and subsequent rapid settlement of the Bitterroot Valley. It is the little-known story of what happened later, however, that brings Owen into the history of Helena, where this once robust and vital individual spent the better part of a decade, essentially hidden away in two different institutions.

Owen was born in Pennsylvania in 1818. Records place him near Fort Hall, Idaho, as sutler (a supplier of liquor, food and supplies to the military) of a rifle regiment in 1849. At the right place at the right time, Owen arrived in the Bitterroot Valley for unknown reasons just as the Jesuits were ready to vacate St. Mary's Mission. The 1850 bill of sale for $250 was reputedly the first recorded legal document in what would become the Territory of Montana. Owen (whose title of "Major" was initially self-styled and later officially bestowed because of his status as Flathead agent) was sharply and openly critical of the government and its treatment of his Flathead charges. He was elected to both the first and second territorial legislatures (1865 and 1866), but attended neither. Yet even in his absence, Owen was named a charter member of the Historical Society of Montana. Among the twelve original members, which included W.F. Sanders, Granville and James Stuart and C.P. Higgins, Owen had been the first to reside in Montana.

During the 1860s, Owen worried over his peculiar status in the territory. His position as Indian agent and trading post proprietor had been viewed in Washington as a conflict. Theoretically, Owen was a squatter on land hundreds of miles from "any portion of the country which had been by ratified treaty purchased from the Indians." The death of Owen's Shoshone wife, Nancy, was a further blow and in its wake, as Owen's debts mounted, his mental capabilities diminished.

According to Father Lawrence Palladino, S.J., Major Owen was brought to St. John's Hospital in Helena in 1871 or 1872. The Grand Master of the Masons personally delivered the major into the care of the sisters for safekeeping. Father Palladino claimed that Owen showed no outward signs of disease. Although it was generally believed that Owen's "failing mental powers" were due to alcoholism, Father Palladino contended that "it may not have been so" since he appeared robust but "his memory continued slowly to fail."

Shortly after Owen's escorted departure from the Bitterroot, future president James A. Garfield, then a congressman, passed a night at Fort Owen in June of 1872. He noted in his journal entry that the Major had "lived like a prince in the wilderness," but declared Owen a "bankrupt and a sot." He further wrote, "Since the death of his wife he has rapidly run down and is now quite a wreck."

It was at this inopportune time that Owen was finally given a chance to prove his title to the Fort Owen properties. By the early 1870s, Owen's property had been mortgaged several times and the Land Office was investigating its titles. According to the *Helena Herald*, July 9, 1873, the major had been informed by the Commissioner of the General Land Office at Washington "...that he may file upon the land he claims under Act of Congress of 1858." But Owen was apparently in no shape to prepare the necessary documents. The fort, appraised at more than $40,000, had already been auctioned at sheriff's sale in 1872 to the highest bidder, W.J. McCormick, for $4,100.

Friends wanted to believe that the major would recover, and he was elected to the territorial legislature for the 1873 session. He, of course, did not attend. Owen was shuffled back and forth between the Sisters of Charity at St. John's Hospital on Catholic Hill (which by 1873 had a contract to care for the indigent "insane and mentally deranged of the entire territory") and the County Hospital. Governor Potts wrote on March 12, 1874, that "...the law is not obligatory to care for the insane at the expense of the Territory, but if I can make an arrangement on reasonable terms, I shall do so." Financially dependent, Owen went to the hospital that offered the best deal.

County Hospital must have offered better terms than St. John's, and so the major subsequently spent time there under contract with the territory. County Hospital had moved in 1871 from its first quarters at the Helena Hotel; the *Helena Daily Herald* at the time identified the new facility purchased by the county commissioners as the "old Carpenter ranch, about two and a half miles south of Helena." The paper goes on to note: "It is not generally known that we have an Insane Hospital in Lewis and Clarke." Dr. J.S. Glick, the county physician, reported on March 31, 1874, that the County Hospital had eleven patients. Among them was Major John Owen, suffering from "dementia."

Fort Owen, where the major lived "like a prince."

At the end of January 1877, during the 10th Session of the Territorial Legislature, it was reported that Sister Josephine had agreed to Governor Potts' request to keep "three insane persons," including John Owen, confined at St. John's Hospital until "such time as other provisions are made for them." Her charge was nine dollars per week, which included all medical and living expenses. This was a lesser figure than that charged by the county hospital—and no doubt a fair charge. But Potts was apparently unwilling to dip into the territorial coffer for the likes of John Owen; his stay was short-lived.

While in the care of the sisters this time, Father Palladino baptized Major Owen "conditionally and privately, his mind being defective," on February 15, 1877, during a "lucid interval." Despite the promise of Governor Potts to reimburse St. John's at the rate of nine dollars per week for his care, Father Palladino—writing in 1924—insisted that the hospital received no recompense.

In the meantime, House Bill No. 1, "an Act to establish and maintain a hospital for the insane, and otherwise provide for the insane of the Territory," had unanimously passed and been sent to Governor Potts for consideration. The bill was approved on February 16, 1877, the very day that the legislature adjourned. The bill contained the following clause: "…whenever, in judgment of the governor, it is desirable to send such insane person to friends out of the territory, he may do so at the expense of the territory...." Owen's Montana days were at an end.

The following morning, February 17, Major Owen was escorted (or more correctly, deported) from the territory in the company of Tenth Legislative Assembly President W.E. Bass, a longtime close friend. Following an arduous journey by stage and rail, Bass handed Major Owen over to relatives in Philadelphia. Just a few weeks later, on April 1, thirteen indigent mentally incompetent patients were admitted to the privately owned hospital at Warm Springs to be cared for under a new contract with the territory for a dollar a day per patient.

So, did Governor Potts do Major Owen a disservice or a favor in effecting deportation? Owen's treatment by the territory has been viewed in a decidedly unfavorable light by Seymour Dunbar and Paul Phillips, the editors of Owen's letters and journals published in 1927. They would argue that when the man who had fought and planned for the welfare of Montana "...had become a care upon the new generation that had followed him, he was not wanted." Perhaps, just perhaps, Governor Potts (or whoever was responsible for authorship of the bill) saw to the inclusion of the deportation clause for a more honorable reason, and made sure that this almost-native son was in the care of a capable friend for the journey back east.

John Owen quietly lived out the rest of his life away from his beloved fort, probably a victim of what we now know as Alzheimer's Disease or some other equally progressive and debilitating infirmity. He died in 1889, the year Montana achieved statehood. In the meantime, Fort Owen had deteriorated under the ownership of W.J. McCormick, and its adobe walls had begun to melt back into the earth. In an ironic twist, McCormick died that same year at the fort, killed by a piece of falling roof during a windstorm.

The *Weekly Herald* of July 12, 1889, noted John Owen's passing with the following sentiment: "...Maj. Owen was for a long time one of the most enterprising, prosperous, influential and public-spirited men in this section of the country....In his prime he was a man of ability, culture and influence....The older generation of Montanians will cherish pleasant memories of Maj. Owen as they first knew him."

JOHN X. BEIDLER

BY JON AXLINE

Forestvale Cemetery is the final resting place for John X. Beidler, one of Montana's most well-known pioneer lawmen and vigilantes. Referred to popularly as "X.," Beidler claimed to have been involved in most of the pivotal events that defined frontier Montana. His contemporaries glorified him as fearless, honest, trustworthy, and "indifferent under the most trying circumstances as when relating some story of adventure, surrounded by his friends and companions." He was also described as a liar, braggart and pint-sized bully. Beidler was, in fact, all these things.

Although he was many things in his life, Beidler was primarily known as a vigilante. He boasted that he had pursued and executed "thirty men of the Plummer Gang" and had also supervised several hangings in Helena. Although long a Deputy U.S. Marshal, he was also a customs collector, assistant Indian agent, and Wells Fargo messenger. Beidler also claimed to have been present when John Johnson received the nickname of "Liver-Eating," and supposedly aided "Portugee" Phillips in his epic ride to Fort Laramie with news of the Fetterman Massacre in 1866. Although he was an admirer of Indians, Beidler's actions toward them were often brutal and lacking in any compassion.

Beidler stood about 5'6" tall and dressed in clothes that appeared to be too big for him. In many photographs, he is shown brandishing a shotgun that was several inches longer than he was tall. Beidler also had little patience and could not abide delay. In his autobiography, he said he was apt to become "boiling, you bet, and indignant into the bargain." One of his less savory traits, however, seems to have been a tendency to take things (including clothing) from corpses for his own use. A self-described "terror to roughs," Beidler called Helena his "home and old stomping ground."

One of X.'s studio portraits.

Born in Pennsylvania in 1832, he was one of twelve children of John and Anna Beidler. According to his younger brother, Beidler received his middle initial as a nickname. In order to distinguish his clothes from those of his brothers, he marked them with a large "X." The "X," therefore, stood for neither "Xavier" or "Xelpho" as has been generally reported. After working for a time as a cobbler, broom maker and brick maker, X. left Pennsylvania for Illinois where he unsuccessfully tried farming and later, he claimed, fought side-by-side with abolitionist John Brown in Kansas. Beidler was in Colorado in 1859 and then drifted on to Alder Gulch in Montana after gold was discovered there in 1863.

For a time, Beidler worked as a placer miner before directing his efforts to trading much-needed supplies in the mining camps. Events in Virginia City and Bannack, however, caused Beidler to "quit prospecting for gold and [begin to] prospect for human fiends." X. won his place in Montana history as the eager executioner of Henry Plummer's road agent gang which was then terrorizing the Bannack and Alder Gulch mining camps. Beidler is reportedly responsible for two of the most famous (or infamous) Vigilante quotes during the winter of 1863-64. When George Ives asked Wilbur Fisk Sanders for more time to write his mother and sister, Beidler, who was guarding the prisoner, shouted, "Sanders, ask him how much time he gave the Dutchman [his victim]!" Also, when asked if he felt anything when he hanged road agent Jack Gallagher, X. is said to have replied, "Yes, I felt for his left ear!"

After March, 1864, X. worked for a time as a Wells Fargo messenger before becoming a Deputy U.S. Marshal under A.C. Botkin. By 1865, he was a regular visitor of Last Chance Gulch, where he claimed to have organized the Helena vigilantes to "try," and execute, John Keene—Helena's first murderer. Beidler's claim, however, is unsubstantiated; nowhere is he mentioned in contemporary accounts of the incident.

An "outlander" and member of the "criminal class," John Keene ambushed and killed Henry Slater at a Helena saloon on June 17, 1865. After his capture, Keene was tried by the vigilante "court" and sentenced to hang. Keene maintained that Slater would have killed him if he had had the chance. Keene was the first to hang from the tree on Dry Gulch. Beidler claimed to have organized the Helena vigilance committee and acted as Keene's executioner. If true, he did this as a duly deputized law enforcement officer. It may have been as many later claimed, that Beidler believed the law of vigilance committee and the rope had precedent over that of the established judicial system in some cases.

In 1867, Beidler's friend and fellow vigilante, Nathaniel Langford, described Helena as "infested with thieves, ruffians and murderers. Shooting affrays, resulting in death...had been of almost daily occurrence." Beidler became embroiled in the cold-blooded murder of a black man on election day—the first election in which blacks were empowered to vote. Although the U.S. Congress had granted blacks the right to vote, the Montana territorial legislature denied them that right. Acting on orders from U.S. Marshal Botkin, Beidler was detailed to safeguard the polling places for the country's newest enfranchised citizens. A janitor named Sammy, who had not yet decided whether he would vote, was killed by a recalcitrant mule skinner named Leach. Showing an amazing amount of grit, Beidler braved a human wall of armed roughs to arrest Leach and took the man to jail (he later escaped and was never punished).

In 1870, however, Beidler's vigilante sympathies almost got him arrested for murder. In January, a Chinese miner named Ah Chow killed John Retzer in Helena. After a short chase, Deputy U.S. Marshal Beidler captured the man, returned him to Helena and then turned him over to the "vigilantes." Ah Chow was hanged and a placard pinned to him that stated "Beware! The Vigilantes Still Live!" Beidler then had the audacity to apply for and receive the bounty offered for the capture of Ah Chow. The editor of the *Deer Lodge Independent* criticized Beidler by stating, "We could not believe that any mere private citizens would engage in so lawless a proceeding and then have the temerity to acknowledge his guilt by applying for and receiving the reward." The hanging spawned a short-lived and, Beidler claimed, desperado-led anti-vigilante movement in Helena. X. allegedly received a note warning him that "We...will give you no more time to prepare for death than the many men you have murdered....We shall live to see you buried beside the poor Chinaman you murdered."

Except for a brief stint as a Yellowstone National Park guide and assistant Indian agent, Beidler continued to serve as Deputy U.S. Marshal in Montana Territory throughout the 1870s and into the 1880s. By 1888, however, his health failed and he lived largely on the charity of friends and the income derived from telling stories at local Helena watering holes. Beidler's exploits became more colorful with each telling, making him a major player in almost all the major events of Montana's early history. It would seem the more frequent the libations, the more daring and colorful the tales became.

Just before his death, Beidler had a number of photographs taken that showed him in western garb toting a large rifle or shotgun. Although he hoped to sell the photos for much-needed cash, Beidler ended up giving most of them away to his friends around Helena. Troubled by insomnia, Beidler wandered the streets of Helena at night and drank in the saloons, until he could fall asleep.

In February 1889, Lee Mantle of Butte introduced a resolution in the last territorial legislature to provide for the relief of X. Beidler. The resolution failed by a vote of twelve to seven. The *Helena Daily Independent* lamented, "Indeed it seems that this general ignorance of the great work done by the most celebrated character of the frontier times...resulted in defeating the measure."

On January 22, 1890, X. Beidler, destitute, died in his room in the Pacific Hotel from complications resulting from pneumonia. His obituary mourned that his death removed "the last conspicuous figure in a notable class of pioneers. The spirit of adventure and not the greed of gold brought him to an almost unknown and lawless section of the country—when rugged honesty and dauntless courage were needed to purge the territory of desperadoes, he became a leader among fearless men."

Upon his death, City Marshal C.D. Hard and Street Commissioner L.F. Evans formed a committee to raise money to pay for Beidler's funeral. The funeral was held in the Ming Opera House and attended by hundreds of Beidler's friends and associates. Wilbur Fisk Sanders gave the eulogy for his old friend, who was buried at Forestvale Cemetery. In 1903, the Montana Society of Pioneers raised a "great rough boulder, emblematic of his rugged character" over his grave. Donated by Kain Granite Works, the stone is inscribed: "John X. Beidler; Born August 14, 1831; Died Jan. 22, 1890; 3-7-77; Public Benefactor, Brave Pioneer, To True Occasion True, Erected by the Montana Society of Pioneers."

X. Beidler remains somewhat of an enigma. To many in the late 20th century, he appears to suffer from the "Barney Fife Syndrome," a small man who was accustomed, by his own admission, to intimidation through the threat of vigilante-style execution. Admittedly, many of his self-described exploits are exciting to read and are told in true frontier prose, but most appear to be highly exaggerated or patently untrue. Beidler was closely associated with the original vigilante movement at Alder Gulch in 1863-64; however, his role in the Helena vigilance committee is questionable (there may not even have been an organized group of Helena vigilantes). Although wildly embellished, Beidler's autobiography is unapologetic in his role in the vigilante movement and there is no question about how he felt about lawbreakers and miscreants in general. It also offers a peek at some distinctly disreputable character traits that characterized this "Hero of the frontier, who took a great part in instituting...the grand civilization."

CHARLES A. BROADWATER

BY HARRIETT C. MELOY

Only limited access to the private life of a public man is available. News articles reveal little about a man's personal character and few reliable early biographies appear in Montana literature. The case of Charles A. Broadwater is no exception. Yet, despite little personal information, he emerges as a compelling study of individual talent and achievement.

Broadwater lived in Montana a mere thirty years, but his

Broadwater Hotel (left foreground) and Natatorium (background) in 1890.

contributions were many and varied. Today, his name is most readily associated with the splendid resort and natatorium he developed and built west of Helena, but his business interests contributed much more to making Helena a financial center that survived its "gold camp" era.

He was born in St. Charles, Missouri, the son of a Virginia planter who moved to Missouri in search of a better farming opportunity. Young Charles received acceptable schooling; then he went to work for a St. Louis firm where he learned excellent business practices. But like many young men, he longed to go west. In 1861 he traveled to Colorado, then turned north to Bannack. As he observed the frenzy of the Grasshopper Creek discovery, which was bringing hordes of people to Bannack, Broadwater's business sense told him to resist the temptation of gold and, instead, to carry food and supplies to the hungry miners. Thus his first career began when he purchased a wagon, bought cattle from farmers in the Deer Lodge valley, and hauled beef to the mines. King and Gillette, major freighters in the area, hired him to bring in supplies from the docks at Fort Benton. From that contact he met Matt Carroll and associates, new owners of the celebrated Diamond R freight lines. His attractive personality and fine business acumen were noticed by Carroll, who made him superintendent of the lines and, in 1869, a partner.

While freighting in the northern area of Montana Territory, he had enjoyed the company of army officers stationed there. These rugged frontiersmen, recognizing Broadwater's executive ability and honesty, recommended to their superiors that he receive valuable contracts for hauling materials brought up the Missouri from St. Louis. The supplies were drawn north to build Fort Assinniboine in 1879 and Fort Maginnis in 1880, both of which were being constructed because the dwindling supply of buffalo meat was fomenting serious friction between the Indians and whites.

Later, Broadwater operated both forts at different times— a tribute to his knowledge of administration and finance.

Meanwhile, it appeared that freighting would soon come to an end, as the 1869 arrival of the transcontinental railroad in Utah prompted railroad plans in Montana. So Broadwater began to search for a wider sphere of activity. His eyes turned to Helena, for here, in the 1870s, was the center of commerce and government. Julia Chumasero, a prominent socialite and daughter of a Republican Helena lawyer, became his bride in 1873. This alliance brought him—a staunch Democrat—into a group of bankers and businessmen. Although Broadwater was somewhat acquainted with the banking industry, he wished to know men in the

profession personally, and he valued his new associates. In addition, Broadwater's business interests were joined with many out-of-state alliances. One of his important contacts was A.H. Wilder of St. Paul, with whom he had become acquainted when obtaining army contracts for building Fort Maginnis.

Wilder backed Broadwater in building a Helena bank. As the freighter-turned-entrepreneur purchased more real estate, mining claims and small businesses, he needed a bank to organize and protect his holdings. The Montana National Bank on the corner of Edwards and Main, built in 1883, was a handsome three-story structure with the carving of a buffalo head over the front entrance; in 1890 two more stories were constructed. Wilder introduced Broadwater to James J. Hill, the Great Northern railroad magnate who was making his imprint on Montana. Legend has it that as Hill looked over the bank, he commented on what folly it was to construct such a large building since grass would grow on the streets of Helena before a bank that size would be needed. Broadwater replied that he would then herd in buffalo to eat the grass. (The buffalo head carving is now in front of the Lewis & Clark Library.)

In 1889, an enormous gold bar—weighing 6,945 ounces—was cast in the shape of a pyramid for Broadwater's bank. Made up of smaller bars from many mines in the Helena vicinity, its value was said to be about $100,000. At today's price of gold the pyramid would have been worth $4,000,000. After the Montana bank display, the gold bar was sent to the Minneapolis Exposition and then to New York to show in the Chase Manhattan Bank.

James Hill chose Broadwater to superintend his rail enterprises in Montana. Two difficult tasks were involved: One was to bring the Montana Central Railroad from Great Falls to Butte. The other was to disrupt the Union Pacific–Northern Pacific railroad monopoly in Montana. To accomplish these feats meant that Broadwater must break his friendship with Samuel Hauser, Northern Pacific's representative in Montana. Broadwater was willing to lose Hauser's friendship because he believed it was better for the territory to have several rail companies rather than one large company; besides he was protecting the investment of a number of prominent investors. Broadwater's place in railroad history was tremendously important to this state, although more of that fascinating story is too long and involved to relate here.

In 1888, Broadwater's last project was formally announced when the *Helena Herald* reported that Wallace, Thornburgh and Appleton were beginning "special improvements" on the Hot Springs at Ten Mile Creek; the "renovation," costing $60,000 to $75,000, was to be completed in June 1889. The formal dedication of the Broadwater Hotel was in August 1889.

A special souvenir edition of the *Helena Daily Journal* gave the following description: "The hotel is a beautiful structure, three stories in height and covering a broad tract of land, built on the cottage plan with broad verandas, lighted by electricity, warmed by steam...furnished like a palace, and has attached to it the finest private bath houses in the world."

Broadwater's natatorium was designed to be the largest and most splendid of its kind in the world. When construction of hotel and natatorium was completed it was estimated that "a full half million dollars" were expended.

Broadwater had hoped to persuade James J. Hill to extend the main line of the Great Northern Railway through Helena, but the road was built through Havre directly to Seattle. The

Montana Central continued as only a branch line, so Broadwater's hope that large numbers of tourists would stay at the Broadwater Hotel and Natatorium was never realized. The developer was not as successful at promoting tourism as he had been in his former ventures.

In 1891 Broadwater's health began to fail. Perhaps his disappointment after such high expectations contributed to his decline. He died on May 24, 1892. Thousands of people from all over Montana and out of state attended his funeral—the largest funeral Montana had ever known. Governor Joseph K. Toole had this to say about Broadwater's death: "I have never known a death to touch a whole community as deeply as has this. Everybody seems to realize that a potent if not dominant factor in social, commercial and political life is gone. No man in this state ever inaugurated and carried to a successful issue more great enterprises than did Colonel Broadwater..."

This man's activity speaks for itself. Even a brief perusal of Broadwater's life and career leaves no doubt as to why he was considered a distinguished leader, deserving of praise.

Harry W. Child and Green Meadow Ranch

By Harriett C. Meloy

Cervantes wrote: "Not every man was born with a silver spoon in his mouth." Harry W. Child was one of those not born to wealth, but one whose achievements accorded him fortune beyond that realized by many of his contemporaries who came to Montana nurtured by wealthy relatives. Harry was born in California in 1857. He arrived in Montana Territory when he was seventeen, lived with his uncle William Child, and worked for the Corrine, Utah–based Gilmore and Salisbury stage line, whose Helena office was located on the southwest corner of Main and Edwards.

Later, in 1875, he tried his hand at mining with A.J. Seligman at Gloster, not far from Helena. A colorful story comes out of the mining experience when Child became manager of two mines in the area. Evidently bullion gleaned from the mines was being stored for financing the Northern Pacific railroad.

Capitalists in New York who were financing the enterprise were too busy to remember to send money to Montana to pay the miners. When the men in the mines found they were owed some $125,000, which did not seem to be forthcoming, they decided to kidnap the son of one of the mine's backers, who had been sent west to learn the mining business, as well as mine manager Harry Child, and hold them for ransom.

On a very cold winter day, the two men were captured. But Child induced the miners to allow him to go to Helena, where he spoke to the chief justice and the governor. As a result, an arrangement was made for Western Union to "open a circuit

with New York to discuss the situation with the financiers."

Money was telegraphed to Child, who arranged with the bank to carry cash or gold to the mine. He returned to the mine by sleigh, taking an unfamiliar route to avoid robbery, which indeed had been planned. His success in the adventure may have led to his being assigned to the Great Falls smelter, where he served for two years as manager.

Child returned to a career in transportation, probably after meeting Silas S. Huntley, a renowned stage line operator with whom Child became a business partner. The two friends married sisters; Huntley wed Annie Dean in 1881, and Child her sister Adelaide in 1883. From Wisconsin, the women were sisters of Dr. Maria Dean, the highly respected superintendent of Helena's St. Peter's Hospital at the turn of the 20th century. Harry and Adelaide Child named their only son Huntley after their admired friend. They also had a daughter, Ellen Dean.

Child and Huntley both invested in Crow Creek Valley land under the Desert Land Act. Huntley, who retired from the stage business in 1878, filed on land between Toston and Radersburg to establish an impressive horse ranch. His large racetrack drew racing enthusiasts from throughout the region, and even as far as the east coast. A *Helena Daily Record* account reported that "horses from that ranch became distinguished on the Eastern trotting tracks."

After Huntley's sudden death in September 1901, his ranch was purchased by the Riverside Land and Livestock Company, among whose major incorporators were Lewis Penwell,

Thomas Walsh, Norman B. Holter, and W.J. Pickette. From these stockholders, Harry Child later acquired the ranch. Broadwater and Meagher county citizens always refer to the site as the H.W. Child property. Under Child's management, the land became a cattle and sheep enterprise, although he continued to maintain a number of thoroughbred horses for transportation of guests in Yellowstone Park, where he was becoming deeply involved in business interests. He also bred small horses, probably Shetland ponies, for underground work in the Butte mines.

While still an active participant in the ranch business, Silas Huntley with F.W. Bach had organized the Yellowstone Transportation Company, probably encouraged by his friend Child. Huntley invited Child to join the business. Almost immediately, Child's management skills were recognized by the U.S. government, and he was assigned to administer the Yellowstone Park Hotel Company. Huntley remained as manager of the Park transportation business until his death in 1901. Child then became president of the Yellowstone Park Hotel and Transportation Company.

Recognizing that more hotels were needed in the park, Child contracted for the services of an architect, Robert Reamer, whom he met in California in 1902. Because Child was highly impressed with Reamer's ability, he invited him to Yellowstone Park for consultation, and the two of them talked of construction plans for several new park hotels. One of the architect's

Architectural drawing of the Green Meadow Farm buildings.

first assignments was to remodel the famous old Lake Hotel. Reamer's drawings promised to give the hotel "a look of elegance." This was entirely satisfactory to the Park Superintendent, who was fond of the Lake Hotel, the park's first. Old Faithful and Canyon hotels were constructed soon to accommodate the burgeoning automobile traffic.

While Harry Child was attaining a national reputation as Yellowstone Park's chief entrepreneur, his interest—piqued by his Riverside ranch acquisition—spurred him to become half owner, with the Gallatin County Attorney, Charles Anceney, of Montana's richest and most famous ranch, the Flying D. A sturdy strain of blooded cattle was shipped to Chicago from the ranch four times a year. When Harry Child died in 1931, his ranch interest went to his son-in-law, William Nichols. Neither of the Anceneys continued to be involved after 1936, and Nichols operated the ranch until 1944 when the California Irvine Company purchased the property. One wonders what Harry Child and the Anceneys would have thought if they knew that, years later, thousands of buffalo would range on the historic land under the ownership of Ted Turner.

Child's ranch interests extended to Helena soon after, when he became an established resident here in 1883. Four years later, Harry Child and a syndicate of Northern Pacific officials purchased the Fant Ranch, later known as the Green Meadow Farm, on the western outskirts of Helena. In 1914, as sole owner of the property, Child invited architect friend Reamer to look over the grassy lands and plan buildings appropriate to the beautiful setting of 5,650 acres. The first, a handsome barn of Swiss design, was built in 1915. It was 450 feet long, its ridge line forty feet in height. Other buildings of the same architecture—a residence, granary, and blacksmith shop all designed by Reamer—"had steep gabled roofs with large overhangs, heavy wood structural members, with native stone and concrete foundations." Many Helenans still remember the barn that had three cross alleys large enough to drive a team and wagon through, and a front loft where dances were held. While owned by W.J. Harrer and Sons, who bought the farm in 1947, the barn burned in September 1956 in a fire of suspicious origin. Not only the Harrers, but all of Helena mourned the loss.

At least three Helena residences also belonged to the senior Childs: 801 Stuart, 706 Monroe, and the Oro Fino Terrace, a handsome Benton Avenue apartment house where many of the Child family visited and lived part time. Harry and Adelaide Child moved to the Green Meadow ranchhouse in 1927, where they lived when not in Yellowstone or California. According to some sources, Harry was most content at the Spanish Peaks Flying D ranch during his final years. Perhaps he entertained friends there, as his fondness for entertaining was well known. He was referred to by friends and others as "Harry Hardup." One writer said he acquired the name because he "made the lemonade and laid out the campsite" for any gathering despite the fact that he "owned a young empire of land and 30,000 head of stock." Another biographer described him merely as "penurious."

On February 4, 1931, Child died at La Jolla in his home state of California. He was recognized as a man who had a keen and analytical mind. His unusual executive ability enabled his successful leadership of the Yellowstone Park Transportation and Hotel Company. This role, along with his activities relating to the development of the Flying D Ranch, the Riverside Ranch, and the Green Meadow farm were admired as contributing to Montana's economy and enjoyment.

RALPH DeCAMP

BY LEANNE KURTZ

A train wreck in Moorhead, Minnesota, was an unlikely catalyst in the career of a gifted artist who spent fifty years sharing his talents with the citizens of Montana.

Ralph DeCamp was twenty-seven years old in 1885 and having a difficult time selling his paintings in Fargo, North Dakota and its neighbor to the east, Moorhead, when he witnessed a Northern Pacific train accident. His subsequent sketches for the court hearing captured the attention of Charles S. Fee, a freight and passenger agent for the line. Fee invited DeCamp and photographer O.E. Flaten to Yellowstone National Park, hoping to document the park's spectacular scenery for advertising purposes. The small party made the trip with a wagon and pack horses. Deep snow thwarted their first attempt to enter the park in June, so DeCamp and Flaten took a sightseeing trip to the still-rugged mining town of Helena. It was an excruciatingly hot day as DeCamp and Flaten toured the placer mines in Dry Gulch. "I wouldn't live here if they gave me the state," DeCamp remembered telling Flaten. He later recalled, "I couldn't figure out how anybody could stand the sun's rays and the breathless air. It was terrible—but the day furnished a sketching for one of the best things I ever accomplished—a canvas that simply radiated that terrific heat."

DeCamp, Flaten, and Fee spent the rest of that summer in Yellowstone, photographing, sketching, and painting for the Northern Pacific all that this new national treasure had to offer. In January, the party returned to Helena, where unusually warm weather had melted most of the snow. "Here's a nice climate," DeCamp recalls telling Flaten, "nice and warm in the winter. I'm going to stay." The next day, the temperature plummeted to 45° below zero, but DeCamp and Flaten were

DeCamp (left) with good friend Charles M. Russell.

broke and had to spend the rest of the cold winter in Helena, eking out a living selling photographs and sketches.

DeCamp returned to Moorhead just in time to say goodbye to his mother, who died in May 1886. Overcome with grief and still mourning his wife Edna, who died in 1880, DeCamp decided to return to Montana, where he had found plenty of subjects for his canvasses. DeCamp was particularly enthralled with the Gates of the Mountains and spent considerable time at Nicolas Hilger's ranch on the Missouri—sketching, painting, and wooing one of Hilger's young daughters. In 1891, Ralph DeCamp and Margaret Hilger eloped, apparently causing quite the uproar at the Hilger house. DeCamp's friendliness and easy manner quickly assuaged Nicolas Hilger's apprehensions, however, and the couple moved into the family's Helena home.

At the time of their marriage, Margaret Hilger was an accomplished artist in her own right, having made music and the study of the violin her life's work. The couple's home became a gathering place for Helena's artists and musicians. Margaret gave violin lessons; and while students were waiting their turns with her, they would wander into DeCamp's studio to watch him paint. Margaret and Ralph had one son, Renan, who is the subject of one of DeCamp's most acclaimed and touching works. "Renan had always wanted a rifle," DeCamp recounted in an interview. "I bought him one. He went hunting. I followed him and I cannot forget the expression of sorrow in his face when he shot his first bird. I sketched the scene immediately from memory and reproduced it. Renan never hunted again."

During his half-century in Helena, DeCamp befriended several of Montana's artists, the most notable of whom was Charles M. Russell. The two joined a group of artists in a sketch club which held its meetings in downtown Helena. The artists all took turns hiring models, and one day Russell brought into the studio a "towering Indian in full war paint and costume." He had paid the model $8 for his services. When DeCamp asked Russell where he had found his subject, Russell replied, "He is my roommate. I painted him up and threw on the decorations. He and I are going to eat on that $8 next week." Russell and DeCamp became good friends, taking numerous trips into the mountains to camp and paint. They had distinctly different styles (DeCamp rarely painted humans or animals), but maintained a fond respect for each other's work. Russell used to say that DeCamp could paint sagebrush so you could smell it, and once commented, "that old boy can sure paint the wettest water. You can hear his rivers ripple." The two had talked about collaborating on a painting, with Russell inserting Indians and horses into Decamp's landscape, but Russell died before that work was undertaken. In 1930, after Russell's death, DeCamp restored one of his late friend's paintings, "Finding the Trail," that had been damaged by a fire in Helena's Harvey Hotel.

DeCamp's rippling rivers can be heard today in Montana's capitol building. In 1912, DeCamp was commissioned to paint six panels for the law library, then located in the capitol. In 1926, he painted four more. A trip to what is now room 312-2 in the capitol serves as a tour of Montana through DeCamp's eyes. Each panel is 4 feet by 8 feet, and the room's high ceilings and skylights allow in natural light that enhances DeCamp's portrayal of scenes from all across his beloved adopted state. The paintings include: "The Bitter Root," inspired by a scene near Hamilton just after a spring shower; "Flathead Lake"; "Above Timberline," depicting a view near the northeastern corner of Yellowstone Park; "West Gallatin"; "The Gate of the Mountains"; "Last Chance," showing prospectors engaged in placer mining with Mount Helena in the background; the Rosebud River near East Rosebud Lake in Carbon County; "Holter

Dam"; a scene near St. Ignatius Mission on the Flathead Reservation; and, finally, "Lake McDermott," a small lake in Glacier Park. In addition to these most visible of his works, numerous paintings and sketches bearing DeCamp's signature are scattered throughout the country.

In 1934, Margaret DeCamp died of a stroke, and Ralph left Helena to live with Renan, an electrical engineer for Westinghouse, and his wife in Chicago. Two years later, on May 27, 1936, DeCamp died and was buried in Helena's Forestvale Cemetery next to Margaret.

The hundreds of Montana scenes DeCamp left behind show a profound sensitivity and love for a place many residents often take for granted. With his soft, colorful landscapes, DeCamp accomplished what even the best of photographers with high-tech equipment are hard-pressed to do: he not only captured the physical panorama before him, but poured onto the canvas his sensitivity and passion for a place he had called home for the majority of his life. He once said he wouldn't live in Montana if he was given the state. The state is grateful he changed his mind.

DeCamp sketching near Helena around the 1890s.

MONTANA HISTORICAL SOCIETY

MYSTERIES

Bertie Miller: Helena's Cross-Dressing Footpad

By Dave Walter

With the numerous excitements of the past few weeks—holdups, shootings, and assaults—Helena is getting to be a dangerous rival of Butte.
Helena Daily Independent, *October 20, 1891*

The crime wave took Helena by surprise in October 1891—for the community believed itself above such things. A rash of night stickups and shootings on the streets of the temporary state capital rendered its almost-14,000 residents shocked, terrified, and vengeful. The streets of Helena no longer seemed safe for honest citizens.

On Tuesday night, October 6, at about midnight, a thief had emerged from the darkness and—brandishing two large revolvers—stuck up Thomas F. Richardson, a conductor for the Montana Central Railway, at the corner of Ewing Street and Seventh Avenue. The robber escaped with several dollars in silver, some change, and a valuable gold watch. The next morning's *Helena Daily Independent* described the robber as "a young, thickset man about 5-foot, 7-inches in height, with a small moustache and about a week's growth of beard on his face. He was well-dressed in dark clothes and wore a black slouch hat."

On Wednesday night, on the corner of Shiland and Broadway, the same bandit accosted Robert W. Ray, a teamster who lived at 1012 Breckenridge. The footpad (a highwayman, or robber, who works on foot) demanded that the startled Ray throw up his hands. He then put a nickel-plated pistol to the victim's head and relieved him of several dollars and a silver

Above: Bertie Miller as herself.
Right: Bertie as "Charlie" Miller.

watch, escaping into the darkness.

On the same night, police officer John J. Grogan—making his regular east-side foot patrol—encountered a man standing in the darkness near the corner of Ewing and Eighth Avenue. He approached the fellow and asked him his business in the neighborhood. Still silent, the chap pulled a pistol, and the two men grappled for the gun. The man then drew a second revolver and shot officer Grogan in the chest. The assailant ran into the darkness—dropping the weapon over which the two had struggled—and escaped.

A bleeding Grogan stumbled to Katherine Carpenter's boarding house at 217 Eighth Avenue and collapsed in the doorway. Soon Mrs. Carpenter and her tenants were comforting the policeman on a sitting-room couch and had called for both Dr. Edwin S. Kellogg and Catholic priest Lawrence B. Palladino. Dr. Kellogg thought that Grogan would recover from his wound, but advised against moving him from the boarding house.

The Helena city police force and the Lewis and Clark County sheriff's men responded quickly. Early Thursday morning they began checking any suspicious person trying to leave town. And then they got lucky.

To the two Helena policemen who detained the slight, young man near the Northern Pacific Railroad yards, it seemed a routine encounter. The fellow—sporting short hair, a smooth face, and baggy clothes—had been picking his way along the tracks toward East Helena. However, he became very nervous upon seeing the officers approach.

When questioned by the policemen, the lad replied in a falsetto voice that his name was "Charlie Miller" and that he

---

THE STORY OF THE PHOTOGRAPHS

On October 8, 1891, authorities captured Bertie Miller and Henry Clark and imprisoned them in the city jail and the county lockup, respectively. The *Helena Daily Journal* immediately sent a sketch artist to the jail cells to capture the images of these notorious brigands. Two rather primitive line drawings of the suspects ran in the *Journal*'s October 9 edition.

The *Helena Daily Herald* noted (October 10, 1891): "Clark was heartily disgusted on viewing a reputed portrait of himself printed in a morning paper. He said that he would willingly sit for a photograph by a reputable artist. The woman, Bertie Miller, also stated that she had no objection to having her picture taken."

Russell H. Beckwith, an enterprising young photographer with a studio at 16 North Main, arranged with authorities to take the pictures on October 15. Because the police would not release Clark, Beckwith arrived at the county jail and photographed the prisoner standing in his cell.

Bertie Miller, however, was permitted to walk over to Beckwith's gallery, under police guard. Against the studio background, Beckwith took several shots of her in the men's clothing that she had worn at the time of her arrest. After changing

---

was looking for work at the new East Helena smelter. A search of his pockets produced an expensive gold watch. The timepiece fit the description of the watch stolen from conductor Richardson on Tuesday night. On this evidence the officers arrested Charlie and escorted him to the Helena City Jail (adjacent to City Hall, on the southwest corner of West Main and West Bridge streets).

A further search of the suspect's clothing at the jail revealed an even more remarkable fact: "Charlie Miller" was really a full-grown woman! A detective exclaimed (*Helena Weekly Journal*, October 15, 1891), "Why, you are a woman!" And Charlie replied, with a good deal of facetiousness, "Well, it took you a good while to find that out!"

Thus began the unraveling of one of the strangest stories in the annals of Helena crime—the tale of Bertie Miller, the

into the gray cashmere dress she would wear to court, Bertie reappeared for a final studio photograph. These are the extant images of Bertie and Henry that appear in these pages.

The *Helena Daily Independent* discussed the peculiar situation (October 20, 1891):

> *Bertie Miller thinks that she has good grounds for a kick. And almost everybody that knows what it is about thinks that she is pretty nearly right. The enterprising photographer [Beckwith] who secured pictures of her and Clark is reaping a rich harvest from the sale of the same. Just where the girl profits from this scheme nobody has been able to discover. She has received only one copy of each picture.*
>
> *It is, of course, customary for officers of the law to have prisoners' pictures taken—to aid in subsequent identifications. However, Helena is the first case on record where a prisoner has been allowed to sit for photographs for the purpose of private speculation.*

On the other hand, without Russell Beckwith's enterprising spirit and Bertie Miller and Henry Clark's willingness, we would not today have any timely illustrations of these two remarkable footpads.

cross-dressing footpad. The terror that had gripped Helena for three long days quickly became a community-wide preoccupation with this strange, titillating character. And the tale rapidly spread to newspapers across the country.

The suspect—by this time calling herself "Bertie Miller," although still dressed in men's clothes—unsuspectingly contributed to the authorities' next break. Just after noon on Thursday, she penned a note and asked that officers deliver it to her companion in their rented room in a small, white, framed house at 104 Ewing (just to the west of Courthouse Square, beside the Alden Block, now called the Courtland Apartments). The note, written in Norwegian, read: "Henry Clark—I am in jail. Come to me immediately. Charlie Miller."

City detective Nils P. Walters carried the note to Clark's room, while a dozen lawmen surrounded the dwelling. The sleeping Clark offered no resistance—even when Walters' search of his room revealed a nickel-plated revolver, several caches of .38 and .44-caliber shells, and a black mask with eye holes cut in it. Within the hour, the detective escorted Clark from the city jail to Mrs. Carpenter's boardinghouse. Here a weak Officer Grogan definitely identified the 24-year-old Clark as his assailant on the preceding night.

Unlike Bertie—who was talking to just about anyone who would listen—Henry Clark remained silent in his cell. The *Helena Daily Herald* (October 9, 1891) described him as "a man of medium height and a weight of about 150 pounds. He has a freckled face and a dark, reddish mustache, is well-built and muscular. But he is very much scared, and he appeared glad to get into one of the cells."

Clark smoked his pipe almost continuously and kept his own counsel. During the afternoon, a crowd of more than 150 men and boys gathered in front of the city jail. They milled about and talked loudly of Montana vigilantes, Helena's former Hanging Tree, "real justice," and "Helena tradition."

City police responded to this threat. Under heavy guard, they slipped Clark out the back door, on Clore Street, and whisked him to the more substantial county jail (then in the old Presbyterian Church, on the corner of Ewing and Fifth, just north of the new Lewis and Clark County Courthouse).

Meanwhile, Mayor Theodore H. Kleinschmidt—in true "Gunsmoke" fashion—faced the mob from the top step of city hall and threatened (*Independent,* October 10, 1891): "We propose to hold this prisoner just as long as we have a man left. The first person who makes a step to break into the jail will get the worst of it." The mayor's diversionary tactic proved effective, and a potential lynch mob became a crowd of curiosity-seekers.

Henry Clark, 1891.

Over the next several days, Bertie Miller worked to resolve her gender. The *Independent* reported (October 10, 1891): " 'Charlie,' or 'Bertie,' while in her cell at the city jail alternatively cried like a woman and blustered around like a reckless tough, boasting of her deeds."

When asked if she would like women's clothing to wear, she responded: "No. It has been a year since I began dressing as a boy, and I have no woman's clothes now. Besides, if I put on women's clothing, I will break down and make a fool of myself. I want to go into court with these men's clothes on, and then I can face them all. But, if I get out of this scrape, I'll put on women's clothing again and keep wearing it."

At an arraignment hearing for Bertie Miller and Henry Clark on October 10, Judge Junius G. Sanders appointed Joseph W. Kinsley as her attorney. The bright young lawyer immediately engaged in lengthy consultation with Bertie in her cell. He emerged with the announcement that Bertie, thereafter, would don only women's clothing. He also asked a number of "the charitable ladies of Helena" to call on Bertie in her cell "to divert her mind from her situation." The cross-dressing foot-pad immediately became a cause celebre for the do-good leaders of women's clubs and church auxiliaries in the city.

By Sunday morning, Bertie was attired in conventional female attire (*Independent*, October 11, 1891):

The dress was a gray cashmere with black velvet collar and cuffs, and the usual high shoulders and puffed sleeves. A white handkerchief was fastened over the little window of the cell while the transformation was going on. When the change was made, the door was opened. The boy had disappeared and instead there was a woman—and a rather pretty one, too, but for the short hair. The prisoner loomed up rather large in her new raiment and acted somewhat awkwardly.

Attorney Kinsley confided to an *Independent* reporter (October 11, 1891):

My client must have a hat, and a becoming one too. When she goes into the courtroom, spectators will behold a stunning-looking female who will change some preconceived ideas as to the appearance of a female bandit.

The hat will partly conceal the blonde hair, cut pompadour. And the bright colors of the bonnet, and the dress, and the other fetching touches—put on by skilled female hands—will transform this tanned boy-ish-looking "hands up" individual into a comely young woman. She will be attractive enough to melt the heart of any stout-hearted juror. In such an array, it would be hard to convince anyone that the woman ever played the part of the brigand.

At the preliminary hearing on October 13, Helena women packed the courtroom and the halls outside. County Attorney Cornelius B. Nolan charged Bertie with complicity in the robbery of conductor Richardson and bound her over for trial. The prosecutor charged Henry Clark with highway robbery against Robert W. Ray. The state selected this offense because it carried a possible life sentence—a more severe penalty than the sentence for shooting Office Grogan. Bail for each of the suspects was set at $5,000.

While awaiting trial, Bertie Miller told reporters bits and pieces of the fascinating story of her fall into crime. She revealed that her real name was Bertha Helen Forslund and that she had been born in Norway in 1871. She had immigrated with her parents to Minnesota as a child and then moved with them to a ranch near Lockwood, Washington—about twenty-two miles from Spokane—in 1888.

Bertie said that she had met Clark when he worked at an adjacent ranch about three years ago. He courted her and proposed to her, but she refused to marry him—saying that she was too young and that her father needed her on the ranch. Finally in the summer of 1890, she took a job at the Eagle Hotel in Spokane, and Clark followed her there.

In December 1890, Clark convinced her that they should try Montana, where wages were higher and good jobs more plentiful. At this point Clark persuaded her that, as two workingmen, they could travel and live together in greater safety. He provided her with male clothing and helped her to cut her hair short. He also christened her "Charlie Miller" when she put on pants. Bertie had not resorted to women's clothing from the time she had arrived in Montana until she was jailed.

Bertie first worked as a clerk in the Grand Hotel in Missoula—for $45 per month—and then in the All Nations Saloon there as a bartender. Clark found employment in Missoula as a steam fitter and, in the spring, he took a smelter job in Anaconda. Bertie soon joined him in Butte. At this point Clark accelerated his holdup career, and the easy money and the danger drew her into the business.

Prior to reaching Helena on October 1, the couple had held up both men and women in several western Montana communities. Authorities found a partial accounting among Bertie's effects in their rented room (*Independent*, October 10, 1891): "Philipsburg, $85; Missoula, $27; Butte, $200+; Anaconda, $58.65 and a gold watch."

In Helena, Bertie was roaming the newer upper-west-side neighborhood, while Henry Clark worked the east side. Although she had robbed no one in the capital city, she did accompany Clark when he held up conductor Richardson, as well as when he shot officer Grogan. Clark had given her Richardson's watch on Wednesday, which the two policemen had confiscated on Thursday.

On October 29, district-court Judge William H. Hunt tried Henry Clark on the charge of highway robbery. The suspect "was cleanly shaven, and his hair was carefully brushed. He wore the same dark stripped suit in which he was dressed at his preliminary examination and at the time of his arrest. He kept his left hand up to his face, and he watched the proceedings, glancing furtively about. He looked exceedingly small and not at all formidable (*Herald*, October 29, 1891)."

Both conductor Richardson and Officer Grogan adamantly identified Clark as their assailant. When the accused did not testify in his own behalf, the jury quickly found him "guilty as charged of highway robbery." Judge Hunt then sentenced him to forty years of hard labor in the Deer Lodge state prison.

"In the afternoon there was a greater crowd than ever to witness the trial of Bertie Miller, alias Helen Forslund, alias Charlie Miller. The ladies were out in force and occupied most of the available space within the courtroom railing (*Herald*, November 2, 1891)."

Evidence presented at the trial cleared Bertie of any complicity in the holdup of conductor Richardson. Clark returned to court to testify for the defense. He asserted that his traveling companion had played no role in the crimes he committed.

After short deliberation, the jury found Bertie "not guilty." The *Independent* observed (November 3, 1891): "When the jury brought in the verdict, the defendant looked as if a ton had been lifted off her shoulders. She stood up, bowed to the jury and said, 'Gentlemen, I thank you for your verdict'."

The *Herald* countered (November 3, 1891):

> *The so-called highwaylady, who has given Helena so much notoriety during the past month through the Eastern press, will go free. It is worthy of remark in this connection that the trial excited more interest than has ever been manifested in this city in a judicial pro-*

ceeding. The courtroom was constantly crowded to the limit of its capacity, and a considerable portion of the spectators were ladies. How far they may have influenced the jury is a matter of conjecture only.

Bertie left the courtroom in the company of Mrs. Robert N. Adams, from the local Women's Christian Temperance Union chapter. Mrs. Adams had befriended the young footpad throughout her ordeal and would care for Bertie until her sister could arrive from Minneapolis.

Bertie Miller visited Henry Clark for fifteen minutes in the county jail the next morning. She then boarded a Northern Pacific express to return with her sister to her parents' ranch near Spokane. An *Independent* newsman accompanied her to the station and reported (November 8, 1891):

She wishes to pass the remainder of her days as a woman. She thinks that her experience in Montana is enough for one lifetime. As a boy, Bertie Miller had opportunities that, as a woman, she could never have possessed: judging life among the vicious classes of society. She says, "A man can fall pretty low. But never so low that there is not a chance for redemption. But when a woman begins going down, there is no stopping the slide, and there is no way back up."

At the depot, Bertie told a *Helena Daily Journal* stringer that she harbored mixed feelings about the five weeks she had spent in Helena (*Weekly Journal*, November 12, 1891):

I feel good, and I feel bad. I feel good, of course, because of being given my liberty. And I feel good because of my acquittal from a criminal offense. And finally I feel good because of the prospects of a happy return to my parents.

But I also feel bad. It will be hard to return home with such a stain on my character. And I feel bad because Henry Clark received such a severe sentence.

However, Bertie Miller—that is, Helen Forslund—apparently kept her word and her resolve. After spending a short period with her parents, she removed to Portland, Oregon. Here she became a mainstay of the local Salvation Army contingent, under the name of "Sister Bertie." A reporter with Montana experience recognized her on a Portland street corner in 1896, but she refused an interview with him.

And perhaps Bertie's story has a happy ending. For, Montana Governor Joseph K. Toole pardoned Henry Clark on Christmas Day, 1902—after the highwayman had served more than ten years of his forty-year term. Toole explained that the original sentence was excessive and that Clark had proven a model prisoner at Deer Lodge. The *Anaconda Standard* (December 21, 1902) observed:

> *Helen Forslund never ceased to work for Clark's release. And there is an idea that it is largely due to her efforts that Clark is to receive what—to a man in his position—is the best Christmas gift that he could get.*

One would like to think that this remarkable story of Helena's cross-dressing footpad and her accomplice did, indeed end romantically—somewhat in the following fashion:

As the Northern Pacific mainliner pulled into the Spokane station, a tired, short man in his mid-thirties stepped down onto the platform. Into his arms rushed a slim woman with slightly mannish features and tears in her eyes. The two embraced silently as other passengers passed them by.

THE MURDER
OF JOHN HANCOCK

ᘛᘚᘛᘚ

BY DAVE WALTER

Like most communities, Helena has been the home of some strange "unsolved mysteries." Indeed, not all of Helena's crimes have been solved and the criminals punished. Even when evidence abounds and authorities develop several prime suspects, sometimes justice is not served.

Just such a case is the 1909 murder of John Hancock at the front door of St. John's Hospital on Catholic Hill. The *Montana Daily Record* called the deed (January 16, 1909) "...one of the most shocking, premeditated, cold-blooded, and dastardly assaults ever attempted in Lewis and Clark County." Helena's other daily, the *Helena Independent*, proclaimed (January 18, 1909): "Few crimes have attracted such widespread attention, or posed such universal comment, or aroused such intense feeling in Helena as the Hancock murder." Since authorities never prosecuted anyone for the murder, the Hancock case remains one of Helena's prime "unsolved mysteries."

John Hancock was forty years old at the time of his death. He had been born in Boston and arrived in Montana with his parents in 1877. John was employed as a miner in Butte in 1898, when he married Clara Hogeland. Shortly thereafter the couple moved to Helena, where John worked for the LaCasse brothers at the French Bar Gold Mining and Milling Company. He also prospected and speculated with partners on York and Unionville properties.

The Hancocks resided in several homes on Helena's east side. In 1903 their son Sidney was born at 514 Eighth Avenue. By the winter of 1908-1909, the family was living at 533 South Rodney, a modest, one-story duplex well up the hill. John Hancock's fellow miners had chosen him president of the Mount Helena Miners' Union in 1905 and, in the fall of 1908, he had been elected to that group's finance committee by the widest margin ever. The *Independent* remarked (January 17, 1909):

> *Hancock was esteemed among his friends and was well-liked. He was not of a quarrelsome nature. Sometimes he engaged in arguments, but they were good-natured. The fact that he held opposite views from those people with whom he conversed did not make that man his enemy.*

Clara Hancock agreed (*Record*, January 16, 1909):

> *...My husband seldom talked of his personal troubles, if he had any, and I never knew of him to have an enemy. He never had any difficulty over mining claims, so far as I know, and he never became involved in any labor controversies....I know of no one who should want to commit this awful deed.*

Yet some "person or persons unknown" purposefully had attacked and killed John Hancock on the night of January 15. As the mystery unraveled, several theories developed.

That Friday evening, John Hancock had left home about 6:30 in the evening and walked downtown to spend a few hours at his favorite watering hole, the Exchange Saloon at 101 South Main. He had returned about 9:00 to find his son asleep and his wife reading a magazine. In his absence, Mary Carter, a sixteen-year-old neighbor, had arrived to stay overnight with her friend Clara; she was reading a book. John began a game of solitaire on the sitting-room floor, near the heater stove.

At about 10:30, the doorbell rang, and John asked Clara to answer it. She spoke shortly with a messenger boy and returned to the sitting room with an envelope for John. He read the note and passed it to Clara, who read it aloud to Mary Carter before returning it to John. The message was signed "Nurse," and it asked John to come to St. John's Hospital to spend the night with a suddenly stricken friend, George Sutherland. John then walked into the kitchen and burned the note in the cook-stove's firebox.

John had known Sutherland since his arrival in Helena in 1898, and both had served leadership positions in the Mount Helena Miners' Union. Hancock knew that George recently had been ill, and he determined to honor his friend's request. He

John Hancock, Sidney, and Clara.

bundled up against the cold night and left the house for the hospital shortly before 11:00. When Clara asked if she should wait up for him, he said, "No, just go to bed when you get sleepy."

John walked down Rodney Street and crossed over to Ewing Street on State. He climbed Catholic Hill to the complex of diocesan buildings and walked around the elegant St. John's Hospital building to enter through its north-facing front-door alcove. The old three-story hospital, razed after Helena's 1935 earthquakes, sat above the southeast intersection of Vawter and Warren, approximately where the northwest unit of the Tower Hill Apartments is located today.

As John approached the alcove, he was struck twice from behind with the blunt end of a hatchet, and he fell to the ground. The *Independent* observed (January 18, 1909):

> *The criminal could not have selected a more sequestered place for the carrying out of his premeditated plan. The place at night where the man was murdered is sheltered by inky blackness, no light shining near the spot....*
>
> *The criminal apparently awaited his victim in an adjacent alleyway....He probably crawled, crouching and on tip toe, until he saw his opportunity, then dealt the terrible blows from behind.*
>
> *The police say that it was a perfectly planned plot and carried out to the letter. Evidently not one hitch*

in the program interfered with the murder of John Hancock.

The mortally wounded victim lay sprawled in the snow only ten feet from the doorway to the hospital, yet no one discovered his body until 5:00 the next morning. Once Sister Calarissio saw the form from a hospital window, she called for help, and attendants rushed the unconscious Hancock inside. Doctor Ben C. Brooke arrived shortly and ministered to the victim until he died about 5:30 that afternoon.

Hospital personnel failed to summon police to the scene until mid-morning on Saturday. But, immediately both the Helena Police Department and the Lewis and Clark Sheriff's office put every available man on the case. Since Hancock's clothing revealed twelve dollars and his watch-and-chain, officers dismissed robbery as a motive. All evidence pointed to "...a deliberate, well-planned, cold-blooded and cowardly crime." Authorities then uncovered the information that Hancock carried a $3,000 insurance policy, which listed Clara as the primary beneficiary.

On Sunday, January 17, Helena Mayor F.J. Edwards offered a $100 reward to the messenger boy, if he would reveal his identity. Perhaps, however, because the Helena Chief of Police said he believed that the person who delivered the message also committed the crime, no one came forward. Authorities worked with only the description provided by Clara Hancock: "a slight boy, about 16 years old, in a dark sack coat and a brown slouch hat, with a wide brim, who talked in a squeaky voice."

On the same day, the Mount Helena Miners' Union pledged a reward of $250 for the arrest and conviction of the guilty parties. To this sum, Union president Sam S. Walker personally added $50.

Chief of Police John F. Flannery's only real progress in the case involved the arrest on Saturday night (January 16) of one Richard Holt. This suspect reportedly had appeared at the Grand Central Hotel about 2:00 A.M. on Saturday in a highly nervous state. He asked for a room, but then changed his mind and departed.

Holt had lived in Helena for about two years and worked as a bookkeeper in the local office of the International Harvester Company. The clerk had been charged with forgery during the preceding fall, but authorities dropped those charges when he made restitution to the victims. Unsubstantiated "street talk" linked Holt with Clara Hancock.

On Monday (January 18), the Reverend Charles E. Miller from St. Paul's Methodist Church performed funeral services for John Hancock at the Hermann and Company undertaking parlors. The *Record* commented (January 18, 1909):

> *The popularity of the stricken miner, the esteem and respect in which he was held could not have been better attested than by the presence of so many of his fellow miners. On his casket many beautiful flowers were strewn....Mr. Hancock was a quiet, unostentatious man, and the services were in keeping.*

Members of the Miners' Union and the Brotherhood of American Yeomen conducted the burial at Forestvale Cemetery.

On Monday evening, County Coroner Edward L. Flaherty convened an inquest in the Lewis and Clark County Courthouse to determine who had murdered John Hancock. During this session—and the three subsequent sessions—County Attorney H.S. Hepner developed two possible scenarios, pointing to two completely different killers. Notwithstanding the arrest of Richard Holt, Hepner's first possibility involved Sam S. Walker, the president of the Mount Helena Miners' Union.

Despite Clara Hancock's initial statement that her husband had no enemies, on close examination she revealed that John disliked and feared Walker. The two men had been partners, holding a lease on the Whitlatch Mine. They encountered high-grade ore in the mine and split this ore. Hancock sequestered his share in the basement of their house at 533 South Rodney. He then forced Walker out of the lease. Clara testified (*Record*, January 20, 1909):

> *He said to me, "If I am killed, Kid, or I kill someone, you will know it is over this ore in the cellar, and you will know who killed me. I know some things about some people which they would not like to have known....Especially Sam Walker has no use for me, but I am not afraid of anyone."*

Called to the stand, Walker admitted that he and Hancock had argued when "Hancock beat me out of the Whitlatch lease."

County Attorney Hepner then produced an anonymous note—carrying a skull and crossbones symbol—addressed to Hancock. It read (*Independent*, January 20, 1909):

Mr. Hancock—You have been accused of "high grading" [stealing high-grade ore], and we expect some return from your goods. And if we get none, look out. The Committee.

Hepner asked Walker to write this passage twice, on two different pieces of paper. Coroner Flaherty and the six-man jury concluded that Walker's copies closely resembled the handwriting on the anonymous note. Finally testimony turned to Walker's alibi.

It took several days for the County Attorney's office to round up the appropriate witnesses—although some of them voluntarily came forward. The resulting testimony revealed that Walker had been drinking the Wednesday, Thursday, and Friday preceding the murder.

On Friday, the night of the killing, Walker appeared at the Exchange Saloon about 9:00 P.M. Several witnesses—including two city aldermen—confirmed his drunken presence until after 1:00 A.M. To the jury, Walker showed sufficient motive, but his solid alibi of public drunkenness at the Exchange made him a very unlikely candidate.

The second scenario that County Attorney Hepner developed in the inquest sessions involved Richard Holt and Clara Hancock. Holt had been arrested on the day following the crime. Yet the thirty-two-year-old widow became the prime witness during the inquest, in which over fifty people testified (*Record*, January 19, 1909):

The large courtroom and gallery were jammed by her dead husband's friends. With their sullen eyes fastened upon her and her self-confessed paramour, the veil of secrecy was withdrawn from the story of Mrs. Hancock's liaison with Richard Holt. In all of its bitter details, it was exposed....

She appeared wearing mourning clothes. A large veil covered a large hat and concealed her face. County Attorney Hepner requested her to remove her hat and veil during her testimony....She talked in a low voice and hesitated many times before she replied to the many interrogatories, vainly trying to protect her reputation.

Quickly Hepner developed the relationship between Clara Hancock and Richard Holt. She admitted that she had been introduced to Holt at the Lyric Theater about six months earlier and that they had met at several "noodle parlors," at the Weiss Cafe, and at the Atlas Saloon. She denied that she had corresponded with Holt—even when attorney Hepner presented several letters in handwriting similar to hers—one of which contained her picture and all of which listed a return address that was the Hancocks' post-office box.

Brought to the stand, Richard Holt stated that he had visited Clara Hancock a number of times at her home on South Rodney, but that "he always asked Mrs. Hancock candidly if John were out of town before he made his nocturnal visits." Holt admitted that he had made love to Mrs. Hancock. Yet he would not agree that he had said publicly that "he didn't know why, but he was crazy, stinking crazy, about Clara and that Hancock might meet a violent death."

Ten feet from the front door of St. John's Hospital on Catholic Hill, John Hancock was struck with the blunt end of a hatchet and left mortally wounded in the snow.

MONTANA HISTORICAL SOCIETY

County Attorney Hepner followed the same theme when he recalled Clara Hancock to the stand, although she remained steadfast (*Record*, January 19, 1909):

[Hepner]: "Did you ever have a conversation with Mr. Holt that, as soon as your husband died, you and Mr. Holt would go away?"

[Hancock]: "No, sir."

[Hepner]: "Did you ever tell anyone that within a short time your husband would die a violent, horrible death?"

[Hancock]: "No, sir."

[Hepner]: "And that you would have lots of money because he was insured?"

[Hancock]: "No, sir."

[Hepner]: "Mrs. Hancock, is it not a fact that an officer of the fraternal society which insured your husband [the Brotherhood of American Yeomen] told you about six months ago that, for some reason, Mr. Hancock didn't care to carry that insurance any longer?"

[Hancock]: "No, sir."

[Hepner]: "And didn't you say that you would pay the premium yourself, and haven't you paid it ever since?"

[Hancock]: "No, sir."

[Hepner]: "Didn't you also tell your neighbors that you were going to get rid of your old man?"

[Hancock]: "No, sir."

To compound the situation, Richard Holt could not produce an ironclad alibi for the time of the murder. In response to some intense grilling from the county attorney, he could say only (*Independent*, January 19, 1909):

> On Friday [January 15], I was in my room all day, until 7:30 o'clock, when I went down to the Milwaukee Beer Hall for a lunch. I stayed until 9 o'clock, and then I went to the [Rodney Hotel Bar] on the corner of Rodney and Breckenridge [the current location of the Rodney Hotel and Creamery, formerly the Red Meadow Bar], where I stayed until 11:15, when I returned to my room, down the block at 408½ Breckenridge.

Corroborative witnesses could place Holt in the Rodney Hotel Bar between 9:30 and 10:30, but not after that time.

Since the distance between the saloon and St. John's Hospital was only three blocks, Holt easily could have committed the murder at 11:00. However, the clerk at the Grand Central Hotel failed to identify Holt positively as the man who appeared there early in the morning following the murder.

County Attorney Hepner, through some crafty investigation, obviously believed that Clara Hancock and Richard Holt had conspired to take the life of John Hancock—for love and for his $3,000 insurance money. During the week following the murder, the entire community of Helena consumed the scandal, and begged for more juicy details. The *Independent* noted (January 20, 1909):

> *It is doubtful if more keen interest has been taken in a great crime in the history of the city than is being shown in the murder of John Hancock. Last night the courtroom in the county courthouse was filled with spectators to such an extent that people crushed each other. Upstairs the balcony was a seething mass of humanity, and downstairs it was worse. It was impossible to get out, and it was impossible to get in....Among the people were a large number of women, who were in all parts of the gallery and downstairs.*

In fact, Coroner Flaherty adjourned the third session of the inquest, held on Friday evening, January 22, because of an unruly crowd. The mob—which an *Independent* reporter estimated at almost 2,000 inside the courthouse and another 1,500 outside—pushed and fought openly in the courtroom, in the halls, and on the stairways. The din that the mob produced drowned out the witnesses' testimony (*Record*, January 23, 1909):

> *One man was standing up against the railing when the inquest opened. Fifteen minutes later, the crowd had slowly shoved him off his feet and he was lying over the railing on the pit of his stomach. He could neither crawl over nor could he crawl back. He was locked in a human vise. He was too tightly cornered to even swear.*
>
> *After the inquest was under way, the proceedings were interrupted every few minutes by the crash of*

breaking windows and the crackling of bursting doors and crumbling seats, sometimes in the gallery and sometimes in the corridor. The officers were requested to clear the corridors, but the crowd literally swallowed them up as soon as they appeared, and they became part of the jostling, swaying corridor crowd. Attempts were made to close the door, but that was impossible.

After twenty minutes, a disgusted Coroner Flaherty adjourned the inquest. However, the frenzied crowd remained in the courthouse for another hour, believing that the inquiry would reconvene. Flaherty held the final session of the inquest on the following Wednesday (January 27)—permitting no spectators into the courtroom. By that time, the community's passion had subsided a bit.

In that last, quieter session of the coroner's inquest, the six-man jury finally rendered a verdict. It read (*Independent,* January 28, 1909):

...John Hancock died from the effect of wounds inflicted upon his head with some instrument causing a fracture of the skull, at the hands of some person or persons unknown....

As a result of that decision, county officers released Richard Holt from custody. In the end, because of a lack of staffing in both the sheriff's office and the Helena Police Department, authorities never produced solid evidence to charge anyone with the murder of John Hancock.

For example, the "boy in the brown slouch hat" who delivered the message to Clara Hancock never was found. Although police discovered a possible murder weapon—a common hatchet—near the scene, it could not be traced to either Walker or Holt. Further, authorities could not pursue perjury charges against Clara Hancock, although she claimed that she never had corresponded with Holt.

County Attorney Hepner's frustration became anger, and his anger became rage. Faced with a lack of staff to pursue obvious leads, he determined to ask the county commissioners to appoint a special deputy to continue the investigation of the case. Hepner sputtered (*Independent,* January 31, 1909):

Lewis and Clark County should have a permanent special detective—not one who couldn't discover a clown in a country circus, but one who has a Sherlock Holmes instinct!

As Helenans focused their attention on other issues, the *Record* editorialized (January 25, 1909):

Within recent years, there have been several mysterious murders in Helena and vicinity, and the guilty have not been brought to justice. There have been acquittals of those guilty of murder in this county, which the general public have regarded as travesties on justice....

The Hancock case has been a "nine-days' wonder" and, when the coroner's jury finishes its work, public attention will be directed to something else. The endeavor to run down the murderer will be sidetracked, because of the pressure of other business on the time of the officers....

Yet the good reputation of Helena, and the demands of justice, require that no effort be spared to bring the murderer of John Hancock before the bar of a court of law.

Several days after the delivery of the coroner's verdict, Montana Governor Edwin L. Norris announced an additional reward of $500 as an incentive to pursue the investigation. Yet county officials never brought anyone to trial for the murder of John Hancock.

As a result, the dastardly 1909 murder of John Hancock has become one of Helena's greatest "unsolved mysteries." Someone, somewhere, somehow knows the answers...but the years quickly are obscuring them.

THE LADY OF THE HOUSE: GRANDSTREET THEATRE'S GHOST

BY ELLEN BAUMLER

Footsteps that echo in an empty building, a name softly whispered when no one else is there, the feeling that someone is watching from the shadows, a fleeting rush of cold air and other unexplained occurrences like these are not so unusual at Grandstreet Theatre. Many of these accounts have been written up in Debra Munn's *Big Sky Ghosts* and the building has been cited in *Haunted Places: The National Directory*. This outstanding Helena landmark harbors a uniquely poignant history which makes it all the more worthy of its reputation.

Most agree that the eerie events are connected to Clara Bicknell Hodgin, by all accounts a very unusual woman. She was dearly loved by many, and her legacy evidently reaches far beyond her all-too-brief time in Helena. The story begins on an Iowa farm in 1870 when Clara was born to parents of both Pilgrim and Puritan ancestry. When she was six, her family moved to the community of Humboldt, Iowa, founded by the Reverend S.H. Taft. This idealistic community shaped and inspired young Clara, who grew up under the guidance of Reverend Mary Safford of the Unity Church and public school principal Eleanor Gordon. After two years' training in Des Moines, Clara returned to Humboldt to teach kindergarten, a position she retained for eight years.

Reverend Safford moved on and thirty-year-old Edwin Stanton Hodgin arrived on the scene in 1898 as the new Unity Church minister. He was immediately smitten with Clara, but the young woman was not so sure. After a long courtship, the pair were married November 12, 1901. Two years later in 1903, the husband and wife team were summoned to Helena, where

Reverend Hodgin became the fifth pastor of the First Unitarian Church. The Hodgins quickly settled into their new community, relishing the beauty of Montana's landscape. The congregation was at that time struggling to pay for its magnificent new church on Park Street. Within eighteen months the Hodgins had reduced the church's $8,000 debt to $4,500 and secured pledges for the remaining amount. By the end of 1904, Clara had endeared herself to the Unitarian congregation and the Helena community as well. Sunday school enrollment had increased from forty to over a hundred, and even non-members—including the superintendent of Helena's public schools—sought Clara's encouragement and advice.

The church building, originally designed by C.S. Haire as an auditorium/theater as well as a church, was the perfect vehicle to combine Clara's creativity with her great love for children. The Hodgins had no children, but Clara took great delight in the other people's sons and daughters. As superintendent of the Sunday school program, she directed her small charges in dramatic presentations.

Clara began to suffer unusual bouts of insomnia and fatigue which worsened in November of 1904. When her husband returned from a speaking engagement in Butte on December 4, he was alarmed to find his wife unable to get out of bed. Despite hospitalization, she continued to plan Christmas activities and characteristically laughed off her discomfort so that no one realized how ill she really was. On January 14, 1905, Clara died at the age of thirty-four. An autopsy revealed a malignant abdominal tumor, then an incurable condition. The Methodist minister and the Jewish rabbi—as a tribute to her nondenominational friendships—conducted a quiet service that same evening at the Hodgins' home. In accordance with her wishes, her ashes were sent home to Humboldt where they were scattered into the Des Moines River. After a year, Reverend Hodgin moved to St. Paul.

Reverend Hodgin and Clara's parents received scores of letters from all over the country celebrating her life. Her family published some of them along with a short biography, entitled *In Memoriam*, and sent a copy to the Helena Public Library in 1907. In spite of the flowery and sometimes maudlin turn-of-the-century sentiment, a portrait emerges of a truly remarkable woman who "loved her friends almost too fiercely," was idealistic almost to a fault, vivacious, full of humor and extremely compassionate. Her grieving family marveled at what she left behind: "...scores of notebooks filled with isolated thoughts and elaborate plans and outlines for future undertakings, hundreds of cards carefully arranged...and thousands of clippings carefully annotated and systematized...." As a teacher, her classroom was known as the sunshine room, "If she were there the room was always full of sunshine, no matter what the weather." Reverend Duren Ward of Fort Collins, Colorado, praised her character as "rarely rounded, strong and beautiful." Eleven-year-old Selwyn Sharp, a former Des Moines kindergarten student, wrote that "...there is one thing I can remember better than the games. That was her smile. I can remember it better than anything else."

Nor was Clara Hodgin forgotten by her Helena friends. They established a memorial fund in her name and collected $500—a substantial sum. Mrs. Harry Child commissioned artist Louis Comfort Tiffany to craft in stained glass a "small but exquisite memorial window" of a mountain sunset "suggestive of the Helena valley." It was installed in the church in 1907.

In 1933, the Unitarians donated their church to the City of Helena and the building became the new home of the Lewis and Clark Public Library. The window was taken down, put away and forgotten. After more than four decades as the public library, the grand old building was again renovated in 1976 to become the present Grandstreet Theatre. The theater had yet to open when Helena antique dealer Paul Martin happened across a listing of Tiffany windows made before 1910. The list indicated where each had been shipped, and Martin was astonished to learn of the window commissioned by Mrs. Child for the Unitarian Church in Helena.

The next step was to locate the missing window. With the help of some senior citizens and a Civic Center custodian, Martin finally located the window hidden away in a basement corner. On December 6, 1976, one month after the first Grandstreet Theatre production, the window was returned to its original home under the approving supervision of Eugene Sand-

GEORGE LANE PHOTO/INDEPENDENT RECORD

Grandstreet's Tiffany window memorial to Clara Hodgin was reproduced on a poster.

en, Margaret Hibbard and Katherine Towle. The three, who generously donated the substantial installation costs, had attended Sunday school at the church and the window brought back many childhood memories.

Helenans today are fortunate indeed to have such a rare treasure in such a public place. Typical of Tiffany windows of the period, when viewed with no back lighting, it appears a marbled blue. Its appearance changes dramatically with each subtle change in lighting. The dedication at the bottom, which reads, "In Loving Memory of Clara Bicknell Hodgin, 1905," sometimes is strangely illegible while the upper window is perfectly clear. The words look as if a childish hand has smudged the paint on the glass. At other times, parts of the window seem peculiarly highlighted.

There is no question in the minds of most of the folks at Grandstreet that there is some extraordinary energy at work in the place. Whatever doubts stage manager Debbye Gilleran might have had about Clara were soon put to rest. Her job required her to be the first one in and the last one out of the building. After locking up following a performance, Debbye was certain she had turned all the lights off, but noticed one still burning in the women's restroom. She went back in through the front door, hurried downstairs, turned off the lights (more than one, as it turned out, had been either left on or turned back on) and as she entered the house from the stage end, there was a "white light that looked like a shadow, a white mist" on the north balcony stairs: "It was an odd glow that shouldn't have been there." A check the following night for possible causes turned up no explanation.

Most, including Debbye, are convinced that the energy, or spirit, is Clara. It would be just like Clara to play friendly jokes on actors, fiddle with the lighting, carefully fold a child's sweater or hover in the balcony watching rehearsals. This intense, passionate woman left so many things undone and loved life so much that it would be like her to stay in touch. Perhaps Clara, who always seemed to bring sunshine with her, helps make Grandstreet such a happy place for children.

Helen Field Fischer, a Helena teacher, wrote a poem included on the title page of Clara's memorial. It might be interpreted as a promise of her lasting presence. In part it reads:

> She loved her life into a thousand lives.
> She cannot die, for when these lives awake
> And know that nevermore along Earth's ways
> Will pass that eager step and helping hand,
> A thousand lives will rise to consummate
> The purposes her flesh had failed to reach.

If Clara does preside over the goings-on at Grandstreet, it must be with great pride. After all, she has seen the old building—and several generations of children—through many changes. It follows that she would consider herself part of its present success.

GOLD IN THE GULCHES

CONFEDERATE GULCH, MONTANA

❧

BY HARRIETT C. MELOY

One of Montana's most dramatic and productive gold finds in the past century happened a few months after Helena's Last Chance discovery, at a site that is little more than thirty miles northeast of Helena in the Big Belt Mountains. Because of the sudden rise and fall of mining activity throughout the camp's short history, records are few and information sketchy. How to separate fact from fiction is a challenge in attempting to relate the remarkable story.

A number of written accounts agree that the discovery was made by Civil War veterans released from guerrilla leader Stirling Price's command when his Confederate forces were captured by the Union army. Confederates who chose banishment to Montana over imprisonment in the South were sent by boat to Fort Benton. Very soon after the Last Chance Gulch gold strike, news traveled to the East and tales of instant riches lured both ex- and non-soldiers. Upon arriving in Fort Benton, four Confederate veterans chose to follow the river part way and then to strike off over the old Belt Mountain Trail to reach Helena from the east. Washington Baker, Pomp Dennis, Jack Thompson and Woolley Johnson prospected the "bars" along the river as they traveled south. According to one story, Thompson looked down from a ridge as the group prepared to camp for the night. He pointed to an acre of land just below them and said to his companions, "There we'll find gold." His prophecy came true when, in a few months, the fabulous Montana Bar was discovered and developed.

Was Jack Thompson a trained geologist or did he only suspect that the ground he pointed toward was a natural sluice box where gold was deposited by streams when the valley bent and folded during prehistoric times? *The Greater Helena Min-*

Diamond City, circa 1870. By 1943, only the high-front remained.

ing Region, Montana describes "the broad flat upper valley of Beaver Creek, at an altitude of 6,000 feet in the mountains north of Confederate Gulch, as an ancient (geological) feature." The mining journal goes on to explain how the development of a number of terraces cut by various streams contributed to the richness of the area. The "gold-bearing gravel of the gulch was deposited by streams at different stages during the process of excavating the valley in prehistoric times."

Thompson and his party found sluicing prospects in the gulch so favorable that they determined to camp during the winter. After naming the site Confederate Gulch, each man built a cabin. When snow fell, as each of the four inhabitants traveled among their homes, the paths made a diamond pattern. Thus they dubbed the tiny settlement "Diamond City" in anticipation of the large number of residents who would soon crowd in. During 1864, 500 miners arrived. By 1865, the boom was on and the number of miners—some with families—increased to 1,000.

A party of Germans from Pennsylvania (or Missouri), which one particular writer described as fall-out from the Union army, traveled to Virginia City, only to find there were no more claims. They turned to Confederate Gulch in 1865. John Schinneman (or Schonneman) with fellow "Germans" Alex Campbell, Charles Fredericks and Judson Tate found pay dirt in the vicinity of Cement Gulch not far from Confederate Gulch. They also acquired the only remaining claims on Montana Bar.

When Thomas Brown came into their camp and asked for work, he seemed to have an unusual knowledge of gold mining. Brown, a very hungry new employee, wrote in a letter home describing the camp: It was evening and "the signal gun was fired for dinner, and I was told to pitch up an empty powder keg. I was given a tin plate, iron knife, fork, tea and tablespoon and a place was made for me at the table." The table "was a rough board trestle about one hundred feet long and it was set under a shed that was covered with sweet, fragrant spruce boughs. On the table was salt, pepper, vinegar and brown sugar." As Brown wondered where the food was he noticed some men "digging in the ground at the end of he table who brought out three large dutch ovens with smoking hot beans, another dutch oven held corn bread, coffee and tea."

In 1866, the legendary Montana Bar was developed. Records do not reveal how many miners were claim owners. However, hundreds of diggers actually worked the claims and probably realized benefits from their work. Several reports mentioned "Pans yielding as high as $180 each." "Even visiting ladies and children were allowed to pan for themselves and keep the loot," noted another writer.

One legend described how the gold was shipped from Confederate Gulch. Three wagons, each carrying a strongbox of the metal, were moved over the wagon trail to Helena and then to Fort Benton. Every wagon was drawn by a span of mules under the "watchful eye" of the renowned X. Beidler, who accompanied the wagons to steamboat *Luella* for the gold's shipment to St. Louis.

Whether or not Beidler performed any other law-keeping duties is not clear. But vigilance committees existed and one story was told of a method of calling men together to protect their camp. Certain committee meetings took place at a shoe shop. When the toe of a boot, which sat on display to advertise the shop, was turned in a specific direction, that announced a meeting, and men quietly gathered. Law enforcement did not seem to be a problem in the gulch.

By 1866, between 1,000 to 2,000 (accounts vary) men,

women and children inhabited Diamond City. All of the advantages of a city were there: grocery and mercantile stores, livery stables, a depot, saloons, hurdy gurdy houses, and a church or two. E.L. Mills in *Plains, Peaks and Pioneers* mentioned that E.T. McLaughlin, a Methodist minister, together with Rev. A.M. Hough came from Atchinson, Kansas, by way of Virginia City, to Diamond.

Pastor Hough went on to Helena but Pastor McLaughlin remained in Diamond City for three of the liveliest early years and then returned to Ohio.

Panning was outmoded when hydraulic mining arrived in late 1865 and early 1866. The *Montana Post* of June 8, 1867, announced: "On Diamond Bar directly above and north of the city, fourteen two-and-half-inch nozzles eject a stream of water day and night...Six pipes play on a Slaughterhouse bar, one-quarter of a mile below town: one on Wood's bar and as soon as the Duck Creek ditch is completed the Boulder bars will be piped." Water was scarce but ditches dug by hand brought a steady flow into the gulch from the area's numerous creeks.

With water flowing steadily day and night, the community of Diamond City was soon literally swept away. Some houses and businesses were moved to higher ground, but many building were simply abandoned. The practice of hydraulicking improved the gulch's success, but for fewer workers. Some miners joined the rush to Sun River where a gold strike was on. Others viewed with enthusiasm the promise of farming in the rich area to the north along the Smith River and east in the White Sulphur Springs area, as well as in Jefferson (later Broadwater) County. Certainly the Sutherlin brothers' *Rocky Mountain Husbandman*, first published in Diamond City in 1875, encouraged interest in agriculture; they announced that the "land would yield up its riches and, if properly husbanded, become the major source of Montana's wealth."

By 1868 gold-mining fever was fading in Diamond City, although activity in the gulch continued the next two decades. However, the brilliant excitement and drama of mining in Confederate Gulch and its Diamond City from 1864 to 1867 would never be replicated again in any other Montana site.

CAVE GULCH
CLAIM JUMPERS

BY JON AXLINE

Few crimes in the mining camps were as despised as claim jumping. Beginning in California in 1849, claim jumping was a common and often deadly occurrence. A mining claim had to be clearly marked, show evidence of being actively worked and had to be occupied. If it did not meet even one of those criteria, it was subject to being seized by an individual or gang of claim jumpers. Many times it was a matter of perspective. A claim may have appeared abandoned, the owner having temporarily left it to obtain supplies or register the claim. In more than one case, a man actively working a claim was forced off through threats or at gunpoint, or even murdered. Consequently, miners often banded together into unofficial companies to protect themselves from claim jumping. It is not clear how big a problem claim jumping was in Montana; that it did exist is clearly demonstrated at Cave Gulch in late 1866.

Cave Gulch is located on the east shore of Canyon Ferry Lake just south of the dam. Gold was discovered there in May 1866. By June, approximately forty miners were working the gravel bars in the gulch and sinking shafts down to bedrock in search of gold. In July, they organized a miner's court to officially record the claims staked in the two previous months. Although located in Lewis and Clark County (then called Edgerton County), the claims were registered at Diamond City, about twenty-five miles to the south. Now underwater, the diggings were located on an alluvial fan that was about 1,000 feet wide and two miles long.

In June 1866, Jacob Hart, Fred Wickman and a man named DeHaven located a paying claim on about 1,000 feet of ground on Cave Gulch. They were soon joined by two California miners, J.M. Siegler (or Sieger) and J. Hassler. Siegler quickly established himself as the spokesman for the partners, who had banded together as protection from claim jumpers. Within a few weeks, the partnership grew to include four more men. There is some evidence suggesting that the claim had begun to "play out" that summer and was not actively worked by autumn.

On November 14, a gang of reputed claim jumpers arrived in the gulch from Diamond City and staked a claim on Siegler's property. Led by James Hassett, the gang consisted of eight individuals, including George Jones and Mike Lynch. The men immediately commenced building a log cabin about forty feet from the Siegler company's diggings and soon started digging a ditch. Virtually nothing is known of Hassett and his gang. Although rumored to be claim jumpers, Hassett believed that they had honestly acquired a seemingly abandoned claim. One witness later testified that no one had worked the claim for three or four weeks prior to Hassett's arrival. Jacob Hart, however, declared that Hassett and his men ordered them all off the property and then staked a claim. He later stated that only two men were working the claims when Hassett arrived in the gulch.

Placer mining in Nelson Gulch. Protecting a claim could be dangerous for the rightful owner as well as the claim jumper.

Within a few days, Siegler and his companions returned to the gulch from York and reaffirmed their rights to the mining claim. Siegler's partner, DeHaven, told Hassett that they had staked their claim in June and "in the name of God you are not going to take it from us." Hassett replied that "[your] laws are all humbug, and we want ground in this gulch and we are going to get it." He maintained that the ground had been abandoned when they staked it. The stage was set for the tragedy that would follow a month later.

Tension between the parties increased, with neither side willing to abandon their claim. On the morning of December 14, 1866, Hassett told a neighbor that he was prepared to fight for the ground, and that "he had more friends than Siegler did" and "could get all the arms and ammunition he wanted." He and his partners then began constructing a 16-by-25-foot log fort about 100 yards from Siegler's cabin. Siegler's group was "prepared for the worst." In a final attempt to reason with Hassett, Siegler approached the fort and demanded that the gang leave the property. According to Hart, he was reviled by the surly claim jumpers with "epithets more forceful than polite." Nearby storekeeper W.C. Smith saw Siegler turn around and move in the direction of his cabin. As he neared the door, somebody in the fort fired two shots at him, hitting the doorframe next to his head. As Siegler ducked inside, the men holed up in the cabin opened fire on Hassett and his men. Hassett was killed instantly and three others fatally wounded. The gang returned fire, but did not hit anybody in the cabin.

George Jones and Mike Lynch were about 125 to 200 yards away, cutting wood for the fort, when the shooting started. After it had stopped, Jones sprinted for his cabin to retrieve his revolver. After arming himself, he fled for Diamond City among a hail of bullets. Lynch was not so fortunate. When the miners spotted Jones, they also saw Lynch and managed to wound him before he could get away.

News of the incident reached Diamond City that afternoon. Within hours, a group of vigilantes arrived at Cave Gulch and took Siegler and his companions into custody. Initially afraid they would be lynched, the men were instead informed that they would be taken to Helena for trial. The party was overtaken by a posse from Diamond City before they reached Helena. Sheriff Ed Lovelock demanded the prisoners be returned to Diamond City for trial. The vigilantes refused and continued on to Helena where they turned the prisoners over to Lewis and Clark County sheriff W.K. Roberts on December 15. Because the county boundaries were not yet formally established, Roberts eventually returned the prisoners to Diamond City to await trial the following year.

County Attorney John Shober charged Siegler and his companions with the murder of James Hassett in the U.S. Territorial Court. Pioneer lawyer William Pemberton represented the defendants. The trial was not popular with the miners and it took nearly two days to seat a jury. When the trial actually began, the courtroom could not accommodate all the spectators and the trial was moved to Jack Langrische's theater on Wood Street.

Trials in Montana were true spectator sports—in this case, literally. Calling it the "most important jury trial that has ever taken place in our territory," the *Helena Herald* reported the proceedings were packed with hundreds of onlookers who had an "insatiable curiosity" about the case. According to one witness, the circus atmosphere of the trial was intensified with the stage serving as the judge's seat and the lawyers "wrangl[ing] on points of law and spout[ing] eloquence...before the footlights." Both George Jones and Mike Lynch testified in the case. The trial lasted a week, with two days spent on summations by the prosecution and defense. The case was turned over to the jury on March 19, 1867. Within two hours, they returned with a verdict of not guilty; the gallery cheered the decision. The *Herald* believed the verdict set a "precedent that will stand as a terror to any and all men who make their living by forcibly jumping or otherwise wrongfully possessing...property belonging to others."

Siegler and his companions returned to Cave Gulch and resumed working their claim. In July, Siegler sold his interest in the mine to his partners and left for Diamond City. While there, he was confronted by Pat Duffy, a reportedly quarrelsome individual who was not happy with the verdict rendered in March. Siegler accepted Duffy's challenge and returned with a "big pistol." In a scene out of a Hollywood western, Siegler mortally wounded Duffy, who spun around and managed to get off a shot over his shoulder. The bullet struck Siegler in the chest; both men died within fifteen minutes.

Claim jumping was an ever present danger in the youthful mining camps of Montana. The problem figures prominently in accounts written by Montana's pioneer prospectors. The Cave Gulch incident, however, seems to be the only one that resulted in bloodshed. There are, moreover, many inconsistencies in the facts of this case. Although a participant, Jacob Hart remembered the incident in a substantially different way than what was reported in the newspapers of the time. It would seem that Hassett's declaration that the claim appeared abandoned may be true; a fact that was supported by many residents of Cave Gulch. What is not known, however, is if Hassett and his gang were truly claim jumpers or if they were called that to justify the shoot-out. In any case, the Cave Gulch incident is an interesting sidelight in our rich history.

"I Would Like
to Quit the Mountains"

By Jon Axline

*We are all well, but I am worked and worried almost
to death.*

Placer mining is anything but easy. Thousands of men and
women came to Montana after 1862 to get rich quick in the
diggings. While a few made fortunes, most worked their mines
just to make enough to survive. Others, like John Wilson, came
to Montana to make enough gold to invest profitably in other
ventures back east.

Born in West Newton, Pennsylvania, in 1828, John Barns
Wilson joined the California gold rush in 1852. After making a
small amount of money there and returning east, he discovered that he missed the West with its "dangers and difficulties,
its broader views of life and men, its lofty mountains and wide
plains." In 1859, he and his younger brother, James, left Pennsylvania for the Colorado gold fields. The brothers arrived in
Montana in 1865 and settled at Blackfoot City, then one of the
territory's premier mining camps.

The brothers early on displayed a preoccupation with having a back-up plan in case their efforts at mining failed. Consequently, they built Blackfoot City's first hotel to provide some
recourse if they proved unsuccessful. In 1865, they filed a claim
on a placer mine on a tributary of Nevada Creek about twenty-
two miles north of Blackfoot City. John's wife, Kate, and daughter, Ida, came west to operate the hotel while the brothers
worked the mine.

The placers in the Nevada Creek district were discovered as
part of the spill-over from Ophir Gulch and Blackfoot City in
1865. By 1870, many miners had turned from the simpler sluice
operations to hydraulic mining. "Hydraulicking" is placer min-

ing on a large and destructive scale. Instead of the traditional sluice boxes and rockers of the earlier phase of placer mining, hydraulicking required extensive ditch systems, reservoirs and nozzles or "giants" to spray jets of water against the gold-bearing gravel of the stream banks. Labor-intensive hydraulic mines were rarely one-man operations. Gold was generally collected during "cleanups" of the sluices once or twice a month. The Wilson brothers initially worked their claim as a placer operation, but by 1871, they turned to hydraulicking.

The brothers' mine was part of a plan to generate investment capital for use in the East. While boys in Pennsylvania, one of their playmates was a young Irish immigrant named Andrew Carnegie—with whom they remained in contact. In 1871, James Wilson left the mine to invest their money with their old friend Carnegie in Pittsburgh. By the mid-1870s, the brothers, in partnership with Carnegie, controlled the Lucy Furnace, Pittsburgh Car Works, Edgar Thompson Steel Works and the Wilson Walker & Company iron mill. Much of the gold they extracted from the Nevada Creek District mine financed their operations in Pittsburgh. From the surviving correspondence it is clear that John got the short end of the deal.

Hydraulic mining in Confederate Gulch.

MONTANA HISTORICAL SOCIETY

Located on Wilson Creek, five miles east of Helmville, the Wilson brothers' mine consisted of seven sluices, a reservoir and fifteen miles of ditches. The season began in April or May and lasted until midsummer when water ran out. Wilson and his crew ran the mine in two shifts from 3 A.M. until 9 P.M. At its height in 1877, the mine was worked by ten men. John supervised the operation, sometimes did the cooking and was solely responsible for the cleanups. The cleanups were, by far, the most important part of the operation and potentially the most dangerous.

Good help, Wilson frequently noted, was hard to find. In June 1872, he hired a surly fellow named Russell to work the pipe feeding water to the giants. After a series of mishaps and quarrels, it became obvious to Wilson that Russell was a "regular backbiter and bilk" who was "so worthless and mean that no one would work with him." By July, he was forced to fire Russell because, in addition to his other traits, he was a "liar to boot." According to Wilson, Russell tried to shame him into paying him $100 a month—about twice as much as what the other mine owners were paying their labor.

John made it a policy to clean up the gold from the races before the men were paid. He also refused to do it alone—his wife and daughters helped retrieve the gold from the sluices. Wilson was always present when the hydraulicking occurred because the "men can steal if they want to do so...." Indeed, in October 1872 he accused his crew of taking over $4,000 in gold from the sluices before they were cleaned. After 1879, he claimed the problem was even worse because of the presence of a whiskey still in the vicinity.

Although the mine was initially very profitable, within a couple years it became obvious to Wilson that its halcyon days were over. In 1873, when some Helena entrepreneurs began speculating in the district, Wilson saw an opportunity to sell out. Dan Corbin, cashier of the First National Bank of Helena, was interested in buying Wilson's claim. John and James decided to sell it to him for $30,000 (although they would accept $20,000). It is unclear what the brothers intended to do with the money, but there is some indication that John wanted to invest it in another mine on Flint Creek. The deal with Corbin failed to materialize, however, because of the economic depression that swept the nation beginning in 1873. It would be nearly a decade before the brothers would unload the mine.

Increasingly, after 1878, the mine became harder to work

because of large rocks and the clay soil. Annual production fell from $12,780 in 1872 to a paltry $2,200 in 1881. John became more despondent and he once complained to his brother that "I like to mine when it pays, but do not when it does not." The mine's reservoir began to fail in 1879, causing him to fret about his safety working below it. Ditches broke, pipe couplings failed and the weather didn't cooperate either. To top it all off, John felt obligated to hire his younger brother, Homer, to run a portion of the operation.

Not only was Homer a wretched businessman, he wasn't much of a miner either. He frequently allowed the ditches to break and improperly maintained the equipment. John felt he was lazy and spent too much time in bed. Homer also refused the help of his older brother—instead verbally abusing him at every opportunity (according to John). Finally, in October, 1877, he fired Homer and confided to James that he "had better work for wages for someone."

By 1875, the mine's challenges began to take its toll on Wilson. In addition to the almost impenetrable rocks and clay, equipment failures necessitated frequent trips to Helena for repairs or new parts. As the mine played out, the money for new equipment was not available and John despaired of even paying his work crews. The eighteen-hour days and stress over the mine's unprofitability caused numerous health problems that he regularly (and in detail) reported to his brother. Hemorrhoids caused by lifting the heavy equipment frequently prostrated him. The long hours spent standing in cold water and inhaling the misty by-product of the hydraulic jets left him with a minor case of consumption. He also suffered from arthritis and, after 1873, "congestion of the brain."

The frequent equipment failure and lack of gold resulted in stress attacks and depression. Increasingly after 1878, he contemplated his own death and the impact it would have on his family. In fact, some passages in his letters to James indicate he even contemplated suicide as an escape from the nightmare of the mine. In May 1878, he'd reached the limit of his endurance and told James that "I should stop altogether for I am not making the board of the men that I have hired and where I am to get the money to pay them or keep my family is a thought that drives me nearly crazy. My life is entirely mis-spent but alas! it is too late to rectify it now." In August 1879, however, John expressed much pride in his oldest daughter, Ida, who received honors as a member of Helena High School's first graduating class.

The mine continued to deteriorate into the 1880s. In 1880, John recovered only $1,050 from the sluices—a fact he tried to hide since it would have made it impossible to sell the mine. As the mine played out, John's spirits continued to sink. In August 1880, he wrote his brother that, "O how I would like to leave the mine and never see it again...." He relied heavily on loans from his brother-in-law, John Thompson, to keep the mine operating and pay expenses. By 1881, it was clear he could not go on. Salvation arrived in the persons of Charles Clarke and William Raleigh, owners of a mercantile in Helena.

John sold his Wilson Creek operation to the men in early 1882 for $8,000. After a short trip back east to visit his family, John looked for new opportunities in real estate in Helena and in farming. His letters to his brother after the sale demonstrate a new optimism in the future. No longer are there any refer-ences to money problems or physical infirmities (other than adjusting his feet to not wearing gum boots). He purchased a farm about five miles east of Helena from the proceeds of the sale of the mine and the Wilson Walker iron mill in Pittsburgh. He also acquired an additional 640 acres through the 1877 Desert Land Act. In addition to wheat, he also planned on cul-tivating grapes, apples, strawberries and cranberries. Because of the farm's close proximity to the Northern Pacific Railroad main line and Helena, he even speculated about selling lots for summer homes to Helena's well-to-do.

Despite dire predictions about his mortality, John Wilson outlived his first wife, Kate (who died in 1888), and remarried in 1891. At the time of his death in April 1912, the eight-four-year-old was remembered as a "man who was not only a pio-neer of Montana, but one who by the force of his makeup and character, as well as by his blameless life, attained a high posi-tion in the esteem and regard of his fellow men." John Wil-son's letters provide a remarkable account of what the frontier was all about for many—a chance to make a better life for his family and himself in Montana Territory.

A MONUMENT OF TERROR TO DESPERADOES

❦

BY JON AXLINE

Few images of early Helena are as disturbing as those of James Daniels, Arthur Compton and Joe Wilson. The bodies of all three men were photographed as they hung suspended from a dead ponderosa pine–Helena's hanging tree. Although such images are endemic to the frontier, Helenans today seem far removed from those days when justice was sometimes meted out at the end of a rope. The Hanging Tree remains a notorious symbol of the early days of law and order in Helena. It was remembered fondly by the city's pioneer citizens and, even after nearly half a century, they still grieved for its untimely conversion into firewood.

The lone ponderosa pine tree was located near the mouth of Dry Gulch at the southern end of a placer mine claimed by Iowa native G.E. Dibble in early 1865. Dibble came to Virginia City over the Bozeman Trail in 1864. After spending nearly a year fruitlessly trying to scratch a living out of his claim on Alder Gulch, he removed to Helena. The tree was close to Helena's business district on Bridge Street (now State Street) and was the only large tree still standing within half a mile of the mining camp. Also somewhat removed from the main sites of Helena habitation, the tree was quickly impressed into service as an impromptu gallows.

It was during Dibble's ownership that all of the hangings on the tree occurred. Although interviewed by the *Montana Record-Herald* in November 1923, Dibble did not share his opinion regarding the use of his property for such grisly activities. The first to die from the branches of the tree was John Keene, who was hanged for the murder of Henry Slater in June, 1865 (some will remember Keene's skull, until recently, prominently displayed at the Montana Historical Society museum).

The last hanging on the tree was by far the most spectacular, a double lynching on April 30, 1870. David Hilger, who researched the site sixty-three years later, is the boy in the foreground.

Over the next five years at least eleven more men met their ends from the branches of the tree, including Jim Daniels, Jake Silvie, "Frenchy" Crouchet, Con Kirby and a Chinese sojourner named Ah Chow. The last hanging on the tree was by far the most spectacular (according to Helena's early historians) and, in some ways, the most reprehensible. The double lynching proved to be the last held under the gnarled branches of the once-stately ponderosa pine.

On April 27, 1870, Beaver Creek rancher George Lenhart rode into Helena with the intention of buying a hay mower. Somewhere between the city limits and the implement warehouse, however, he got lost in the warren of saloons and hurdy gurdy houses located in and around Last Chance Gulch. Within a few hours, he had arrived at Joe Reed's New York Saloon on Rodney Street, roaring drunk and ready to buy the house a round. Unbeknownst to Lenhart, however, two men had been shadowing him most of the afternoon.

Twenty-six-year-old Arthur Compton arrived in Helena in 1869 after being accused of stealing $800 from a merchant in Salt Lake City. Described as having a pockmarked face and a disfigured nose, Compton worked in a tin shop on Rodney Street. His partner, Joe Wilson, was less savory and spent most of his time loitering around the Rodney Street saloons. Wilson was described as "aside from one of his eyes, which [had] a film, tolerably good looking." While Compton was described as "kindly" by one of his contemporaries, Wilson had a reputation as a "burly, rough and uncouth" individual.

When Lenhart left the saloon for home at about 6 P.M. (presumably without his hay mower), Compton and Wilson hurried to Adkin Kingsbury's Pacific Stables on Main Street and procured two horses. Because neither man had any money to pay for the animals, they signed a promissory note against Compton's wages. Suspicious that the men were trying to escape the law, Kingsbury questioned them closely about their destination. They told him they were going "down to the Prickly Pear."

Later that evening, the duo caught up with Lenhart, knocked him from his horse with a rock hurled from a slingshot and then shot him in the hip (a "lucky" shot since both men had already emptied their revolvers at Lenhart); they then robbed him and pistol-whipped the man into unconsciousness. Although semiconscious the next day when found lying alongside the road, Lenhart was able to identify his assailants who were apprehended without incident later that evening.

Within hours, the citizens of Helena had been stirred into a frenzy over the incident. The *Helena Weekly Herald* stated "Search the records of Montana from its earliest history down to the present time, and a crime the like of this so fiendish, so cold-blooded, will find no parallel…the deeds of Plummer and his band of 'road agents' would, by the side of this, pale into insignificance." At an evening town meeting held on the steps of the county courthouse, twelve men calling themselves vigilantes appointed a twenty-man jury to try Compton and Wilson on the streets of Helena the next day. The "trial," however, was held at a local warehouse where only the "jury" and the accused were present. Within hours, both Compton and

Wilson were pronounced guilty of the crime of highway robbery and assault with the intent to commit murder. Harvey English and Robert Lawrence asked the assembled mob what the sentence should be for the crime. Over the protests of District Attorney John Shober and District Court Judge George Symes, the mob voted to hang Compton and Wilson the following day. Later that evening, the "vigilantes" stormed the jail and removed the prisoners to a warehouse near courthouse square until the next day.

At about 4:45 P.M. on April 30, 1870, Compton and Wilson were taken to the tree on Dry Gulch and placed into the bed of a Murphy wagon drawn up under its branches. By this time an "immense concourse of citizens had congregated, some in wagons and carriages, some on horseback and hundreds standing around on the side hills nearby and on the tops of houses." The arms and legs of the prisoners were bound and their faces covered with white handkerchiefs. When asked if they had any last words, only Compton responded by warning others to "be careful and not lead the life that I have led for the past few days." Compton and Wilson were launched into eternity at exactly 5 P.M. While Compton's neck was broken, the noose slipped on Wilson and the man took over eight minutes to strangle to death. Helena photographer Madame M.A. Eckhart photographed the ghastly scene within an hour of the event. The double hanging was the last held in Helena under the auspices of the Helena "vigilantes."

By the early 1870s, however, Dibble's claim had "played out" and he abandoned the property. In August 1875, Justice of the Peace Nick Hilger transferred ownership of the property containing the hanging tree to pastor William Shippen of the Methodist Episcopal Church at the corner of Broadway and Ewing streets (it is not clear if there was a house on the property when he acquired it; the 1875 "Birds-Eye View of Helena" map shows a substantial two-story wood frame house close to the tree).

In May 1875, spring runoff undermined two of the Hanging Tree's three main roots. The tree leaned ominously over Shippen's newly constructed carriage house on the southwest corner of his lot. Afraid that the tree would topple and kill his horse, Shippen hired an itinerant woodcutter to fell the tree before it could cause any damage. For $2.50, one of Helena's most noted landmarks was toppled. The felling of the hangman's tree caused a near riot as Helenans flocked to the site to collect souvenirs. The tree was not cut down because of the righteous indignation of the pastor as has been popularly depicted.

By his own admission, Shippen was astounded at the reaction the demise of the tree caused to the city's citizens. He clearly hadn't realized the reverence that many Helenans held for that "gruesome old relic." Many people apparently prized the tree for its educational value as a warning to all who broke the law. There was even talk of "subjecting the preacher to indignity" for cutting down the tree. Although it has also been claimed that he cut up the tree for use as canes, that story has not been substantiated. Shippen left Helena later that year and served as the pastor of Butte's Methodist Episcopal Church until his death in August 1911. As late as 1907, however, he was surprised by the anger directed at him by Helenans still upset over the destruction of the Hanging Tree.

The last chapter in the saga of the Hanging Tree was played out in June 1923. That year, David Hilger, John Shober and Richard Lockey undertook a project under the auspices of the Montana Historical Society, to firmly establish the site of the tree. Although they intended to commemorate the site with a plaque, there is no evidence that it was ever placed.

The trio relied heavily on their own memories of the tree and also utilized courthouse records to help them pinpoint the site. The men discovered that the Hanging Tree was located on the property of Jacob Opp at 521 Hillsdale. Jacob, the funeral director at the Hermann Company mortuary, purchased the property from William Shippen in 1876. Opp had destroyed the last tangible remnant of the tree when he removed some roots while excavating a foundation for an addition to the house in about 1913.

For those of you who've always wanted to know where the Hanging Tree stood, it was located on the property line between 521 Hillsdale and 538 Highland, near the corner of Blake Street.

LIFESTYLE

WHEN DIPHTHERIA
WAS IN TOWN

BY ELLEN BAUMLER

In the late fall of 1885 eight-year-old Jennie "Too-too" Brooke lay dying of diphtheria. Even the considerable skill of Dr. Ben C. Brooke, a fourth generation physician, longtime Helena practitioner and Too-too's father, could do nothing to stop the course of this deadly disease.

Typical Montana doctor's office of the late 19th century.

Like any other place where people lived in close proximity to their neighbors, Helena had experienced previous epidemics. Yet, as Dr. Jacob J. Leiser wrote in 1881, Montana was actually a "healthy Territory." Dr. Leiser, an early proponent of public health and a well educated physician, found no disease to be prevalent in Helena at that particular time. He explained that during the preceding year, 1880, Helena could count three so-called epidemics of diseases "peculiar to the civilized world." The first two, measles and whooping cough, claimed two lives each—all of them very young children. The last and most severe was diphtheria which took a dozen victims. Dr. Leiser suggested that "in comparison to its effect upon similar towns in the States, we can scarcely give it the name of epidemic." The population at that time in Helena was about 4,000. All factors considered, Dr. Leiser fixed the death rate for 1880 at 12 per thousand, and only one sixth of those were children. He partly attributed this low rate to the dry climate: "...a carcass in the street instead of decomposing...literally dries up, scarcely tainting the air at all." Helena was lucky to have been so mildly afflicted. But living where an epidemic was generally limited to a dozen or so victims was little consolation to Dr. Brooke when Too-too was so critically ill.

Although Dr. Brooke's preferred treatment of diphtheria is not known, medical authorities of the day had long argued over the methods. The appearance of a tough grayish membrane covering the tonsils and throat, and other flu-like symptoms characterize the disease which most often, but not exclusively, attacked children between the ages of two and twelve. Vapors of turpentine and liquid tar burned on the stove in the patient's room were said to "dissolve the fibrinous exudations which choke up the throat." Solutions of coal tar and lime water, alum and carbolic acid, or powdered sulfur and lime water were considered excellent antiseptic gargles. Drawing sulfur into the nostrils through a quill was also thought to be a good prevention. Nonetheless, diphtheria was fatal in one out of every two cases.

Helenans followed the battle that raged on the pages of the *Daily Independent* in December and January of 1885 and 1886 between Helena's Dr. Moses Rockman and Dr. Ernest Crutcher of Choteau over the latest treatment of this stubborn villain. Dr. Rockman wrote that part of the problem was catching the disease early. He advised mothers to inspect their children's throats twice daily "when diphtheria is in town." The presence of one or more white, yellow or gray spots at the back of the throat confirmed the diagnosis. Immediate treatment was essential. Dr. Rockman's method was to paint the throat with a sponge dipped in a mixture of silver nitrate and water three times daily. Exactly every half hour the patient should gargle with a solution of chloride aluminum. In the case of a very young child unable to gargle, the throat had to be irrigated with a syringe. The mother must follow this procedure, even though it seemed worse than the disease. Dr. Rockman chastised the mother who did not follow these instructions: "…stop reading, this is not for you; you are too chicken-hearted; you have no actual love for your child. Your child will die."

Kindly Dr. Crutcher countered, describing Dr. Rockman's cure as "absurd and barbarous" and admonished his colleague thus: "Honestly now, Dr. R, did you ever see a solitary child with strength enough to survive your…treatment?" (Dr. Crutcher admitted, however, that the sponge could be useful on adults as "it entertains the sick one and gratifies the friends.") Among other things, Dr. Crutcher recommended sublimed sulfur "blown through a long quill or small paper cone—into the patient's throat—This destroys the germ and at least prevents the suffocating symptoms." In the most severe cases, Dr. Crutcher advocated the use of camphor, ether injected hypodermically, caustic potassa, massage and electric shock. To this last list of Dr. Crutcher's remedies, Dr. Rockman suggested adding "requiescat in pace," since in his view, death would be the certain result.

Even Drs. Rockman and Crutcher agreed, however, that diphtheria was highly contagious. By the 1880s, physicians had generally accepted the 1860s discoveries made by Joseph Lister, recognizing that disinfectants and isolation of the sick could help prevent the spread of "catching" diseases. At the first sign of Too-too's symptoms, Dr. Brooke had sent a second daughter, five-year-old Blanche, to the West Side in the hopes of avoiding contagion. When Too-too died some days later, the editors of the *Helena Herald* posed this question: "How is it that the Board of Health did not take cognizance of the fact [that diphtheria was present in the home] and establish the usual quarantine?"

The Board of Health swiftly made its reply. The chairperson at the time was Dr. Maria Dean, a newcomer to Helena who had recently completed medical training abroad. Dr. Dean insinuated that certain citizens had unlawfully removed quarantine flags. She promised prosecution and a $20 fine for anyone interfering with the board's actions. The Board requested that physicians attending households under quarantine caution occupants to "abstain from intermingling with others." Further, "...when a case dies or recovers...see that the bedding and premises are thoroughly disinfected and allow no bedding to be exposed to the public by being hung out on fences near the sidewalks..."

Despite the best intentions, Dr. Brooke also lost his battle for Blanche when she died two weeks after her sister. Within a few days, the *Daily Independent* also chronicled the death of Mrs. E.M. Dunphy, who succumbed to diphtheria after nursing the Kuhn children, two of whom also died. On the same page next to this somber report, an invitation to a church Christmas party was extended to children of all ages. The announcement ended: "Let the church be crowded." Indeed, the public was not so easy to educate.

By the new year, 1886, the epidemic had subsided and those who played key roles in the drama carried on as before. Dr. Leiser built up a lucrative Helena practice, but apparently not lucrative enough, for he closed up shop to follow the 1890s gold rush in Alaska. After ten years in Helena, Dr. Rockman successfully practiced in both Kalispell and Missoula. Dr. Crutcher was appointed to the first Board of Medical Examiners in 1889, moved to Los Angeles in 1900 and died there in 1948. Dr. Maria Dean, one of the first women doctors licensed in Montana, set up a Helena practice specializing in the diseases of women and children. She later declined the offer to run for Congress; Jeannette Rankin ran instead. Helena lost a great advocate when Dr. Dean died in 1919. As for Dr. Brooke, along with a short remembrance of his daughters by their Sunday School teacher, the same page of the *Daily Independent* recorded his divorce in January 1886. He continued practicing medicine until his death in 1891. Ben, Jr., followed in his father's footsteps to become a fifth generation physician. Perhaps the loss of his two small sisters helped in his career choice.

And what of diphtheria? The epidemic of 1885 left more than a dozen victims in its wake, but even as Too-too and Blanche Brooke became statistics, research was ongoing a world away in Europe which would soon lead to the revolutionary discovery of a diphtheria antitoxin. This, the first serum antitoxin to be manufactured commercially, was made available to the public in 1895. The widespread use of the DPT vaccine today has almost eradicated this disease.

CHRISTMAS IN HELENA: AN EVOLVING CELEBRATION

BY DAVE WALTER

We really have not been doing this thing very long. Helenans have celebrated the birth of the Christ child for only 130 years. Yet this particular holiday has developed into our major annual festival, gathering momentum after Thanksgiving and dissolving into the more secular activities of New Year's Day. Through the decades, Christmas has remained not only the greatest of children's holidays, but also a time for adults to practice "Peace on earth; good will toward men."

So, Christmas has become a benchmark: a signpost by which we measure our time; an occasion we use to reflect on our past and present accomplishments and disappointments. The holiday also offers us the opportunity to remove ourselves from the usual chaos of daily life to consider some higher ideals. This season—which entwines the passage of the winter solstice, with the birth of the Christ in a stable, with the tradition of Saint Nicholas in the guise of Santa Claus—always evokes intense emotions in each of us.

Yet the celebration of Christmas never remains static. As individuals and as families and as a community, we keep changing our menus, gift choices, colors, ornaments, and activities. For example, only one percent of Americans ate plum pudding last Christmas; for every American home that included a real Christmas tree last year, another home erected and decorated an artificial tree. How Helenans choose to observe Christmas Day continues to evolve.

With apologies to Bing Crosby, the term "white Christmas" perfectly fits the Montana situation. This Christian festival day arrived in Montana with the earliest explorers, fur trappers, missionaries, and settlers—a custom of white civilization.

Christmas in the 1860s placer-gold camp of Last Chance

Gulch played to an overwhelmingly young, male population. To these transient miners, far from their homes and families, the holiday offered little more than an excuse for an extended drunk, accompanied by violence. An 1867 incident in McClellan Gulch (located west of Stemple Pass, about fifteen miles southeast of Lincoln) is typical of this rough-and-tumble society (Virginia City *Montana Post*, January 4, 1868):

> *A row occurred in Dailey's Saloon in McClellan Gulch on Christmas Eve. In it one man was mortally wounded, and two other persons were severely wounded. It appears that a free and easy dance was in progress and, during the excitement, a "fast" Spanish woman named Rosella (formerly a resident of Helena, who was compelled to leave there for attempting the life of another woman) became involved in a quarrel with one of the men. Then Fanny Clark stepped in and offered to stand by her friend, Rosella.*

> *At this point, John Smoot interfered on the part of the man, and a general fight resulted. During the melee, Smoot received a fearful cut in the abdomen by a knife. It is not known as yet by whom the knife was used. Rosella also received a severe blow over the head with a revolver, and a man named Doyle was badly cut.*

> *Medical assistance was sent for, but the messenger was drunk and became lost in the mountains. Smoot died on Thursday morning, before any assistance arrived. He was a young man, and we understand that his relatives reside in Blackfoot City.*

Helena, like some other Montana mining camps, survived and became a town. Women and children settled in these communities, and brought less violent customs. By the 1870s, whether a Montana town observed Christmas without excessive public drunkenness and open violence became a measure of its social development.

At a time when few families decorated trees in their own homes, the Sunday School Christmas-tree presentation served as the prime holiday event. Usually held on Christmas Eve, this ceremony often included a short sermon, Sunday School classes singing carols, and individual children reciting memorized Christmas verses and stories.

Although not so prominent as he later would become, Santa Claus then appeared, to distribute little gifts. These parcels had been tucked into the boughs of the candle-lit tree. They frequently contained oranges, apples, hard candy, and nuts. Just such a ceremony occurred in Helena in 1876 (*Helena Weekly Herald*, December 30, 1876):

> One of the finest occasions of its kind that has yet taken place in the Territory was the Christmas Eve exercises of the children of the Methodist Episcopal Sunday School. It is one, too, that reflected the very highest credit on all concerned. The old Theater building on Bridge Street was beautifully wreathed in evergreens, and the stage was adorned with a splendidly illuminated and beautifully provided Christmas tree.
>
> The scholars were arranged on the stage, and the pit and the gallery were densely packed. There was a large attendance of the blushing maids and blooming matrons of Helena, who lent a charm and grace to the scene that reminded not a few people of other days and other climes.
>
> The opening exercises were followed by the dialogues and the reading of fugitive pieces by the scholars, who acquitted themselves in an excellent manner. We cannot particularize when all of the presenters did so well.
>
> After this came the distribution of the presents on the tree. Bright eyes shone brighter (even of those often of an adult age) as the presents of friends, and mayhap lovers, were handed to their owners.
>
> After the singing of the doxology, and a benediction by the Reverend A.M. Hough, the assemblage dispersed—the little ones to revel in their present gifts and to dream of Santa Claus, and the older ones well-pleased with an entertainment that will be a green spot in their memory long days hence.

Christmas-tree presentations survived in smaller Montana

communities well into the twentieth century. Likewise, the traditional gift of apples/oranges/hard candy/nuts lasted across the state until after World War II. At the turn of the century, Helenans experimented with a community-wide, secular Christmas tree and accompanying exercises. Although this practice did not last here, the focused community-tree celebration survives in some Montana towns.

Also at the turn of the century, the Christmas practice of caring for the needy rose in importance. Formerly an individual's responsibility, the care of the less fortunate became the concern of private social-welfare and fraternal groups. Since Helena included many institutions—orphanages, boarding schools, hospitals, the county poor farm—in addition to individual families, the community rallied to provide meals, gifts, and provisions for the poor and the needy. Obviously this practice continues to the present.

In this spirit, the local Elks lodge developed a community-wide event for Helena's children. The annual gathering usually occurred on the day before Christmas, at the Auditorium—a magnificent brick building that also housed the Public Library, located on the northwest corner of Seventh Avenue and Warren Street, just south of Central School. The (Helena) *Montana Daily Record* describes the organization's preparations for the 1903 affair (December 24, 1903):

> *Friday morning at 11 o'clock Santa Claus will arrive at the Auditorium to take charge of the Christmas festivities of the Helena lodge of the Benevolent and Protective Order of Elks. The members of that order have undertaken to entertain all the children of Helena at that time. When the "choo choo" of Santa's steam automobile announces his arrival and the big double doors of the large building are swung open to admit his entrance, there will no doubt be close to 2,000 little ones present to greet him.*
>
> *Aside from the candy, fruit, and nuts, a package of which will be given to all of the children attending, Santa Claus has given it out that about 300 of the children of Helena are down on his list to receive some article which will be of use to them afterwards.*

Santa sent a wireless telegram to the chairman of the committee on arrangements, and it said, "I will bring with me mittens, shoes, stockings, caps, and all that sort of thing. I understand there are numerous children in Montana's capital who have, by their behavior during the past year, become entitled to some substantial gift."

The last thing Santa Claus said in his message was, "I hope all of the children in Helena will be at the Auditorium, for I want to see them. I recall the most pleasant memories from my previous visits to their town."

The man who depicted Santa in this instance was A.I. "Daddy" Reeves, one of Helena's most enduring Christmas traditions. He was a newspaperman who arrived in Helena in 1892 and began working in the Jackson Music House. By 1894 he owned his own music store, which for years was located at 19 South Main and called the Reeves Music House. During most of his life, Reeves lived at the Montana Club.

A.I. "Daddy" Reeves circa 1913.

"Daddy" Reeves never married, but he donated countless hours to the children of Helena. He took special interest in the city's newsboys, the kids at the Intermountain Deaconess Home, and the youngsters at St. Joseph's Orphanage. For them he organized harmonica bands, choral groups, picnic outings to local attractions, and activity-filled banquets.

Reeves' music store became a downtown mainstay until the fire of 1928 burned him out. Thereafter he taught music lessons from his rooms at 141 East Sixth Avenue. Throughout his life, Reeves underwrote the appearance in Helena of such major musicians as Ernestine Schumann-Heink, Ignace Paderewski, Lillian Nordica, and the St. Paul Orchestra.

"Daddy's" most notable contribution, however, became his annual depiction of Santa Claus. For more than fifty years—from 1896 until his death in 1951—he served as the official Elks Santa. In addition, each year he worked any number of other private and club Christmas parties. Thousands of Helena youngsters remembered Reeves' performances, and many later brought their children and their grandchildren to enjoy this local Santa legend.

"Daddy" Reeves specialized in surprise arrivals and worked diligently never to duplicate an entrance. For example, at the Elks' 1903 party, he used a real novelty, an automobile (*Montana Daily Record*, December 25, 1903):

> *Presently those on watch at the front entrance of the Auditorium gave the signal that Santa was in sight. And, sure enough, he was. With the whirr of rubber wheels and the hiss of escaping steam, he and his chauffeur rounded the corner of Breckenridge and Warren Streets, flew past the Grandon Hotel and on to the Auditorium.*
>
> *As they neared the place, the double doors of the building were swung open. The red automobile and its jolly occupant glided into the building, beneath the gallery, between the supporting posts, and into the middle of the room.*
>
> *Then the little folks rose up in a frenzy of delight and shouted themselves hoarse. Twice around without stopping the vehicle went Santa, all the time waving and shouting his greetings to his young friends....*

In other memorable entrances, Reeves literally dropped from inside a chimney into a fireplace, and he rode an old sleigh, drawn by four prancing horses. He once crouched behind wrapped boxes in a Montana Club fireplace for almost two hours, before bursting into the midst of a private holiday party of surprised and delighted youngsters.

"Daddy" approached his task with painstaking concern. He

Reeves as Santa at a 1930s Elks' party in the Auditorium.

purchased his elaborate outfit made-to-order from a theatri-
cal-costume company in Hollywood. He always hired a professional to put on his makeup, because he wanted "everything
to be perfect, just as though I were going out to play Shakes-
peare." Throughout his show, "Daddy" cavorted without resting—hopping, skipping, jumping, and capering. In 1938, at age
seventy-four, he explained (*Montana Newspaper Association
Inserts*, January 3, 1938):

> *Santa Claus is a character from fairyland, so far
> as little children are concerned, so I act as sprightly
> as I can throughout the performance. It keeps them
> excited and interested.*
>
> *This routine calls for reserve strength and lots of
> it, so I go into training every year about Thanksgiving
> Day, and I begin by running in place. I do 25 steps the
> first day, then increase the exercise 25 steps a day,
> until I can keep it up for an hour without losing my
> breath. I go on a light diet too.*

Reeves also told of an instance when he sensed that some
older boys were going to attempt to "expose" him, by pulling
his beard and clothing. So he eluded them and outran the entire group. "It was due to my training that I beat them in the
foot race," he said.

Helena's traditional St. Nick continued:

> *The greatest problem in playing Santa Claus is
> how to cool off. Now, when I am through with my act-
> ing job, I am blanketed like a race horse and taken*

home. I get into a tub of warm water and soak for
about 30 minutes. Then I go to bed between warm
blankets and remain there for a couple hours. Next I
take a cold shower. And then I'm ready for a giant
turkey-eating contest!

From 1896 to 1950, "Daddy" Reeves brought continuity to
Helena's Christmas celebrations. In the meanwhile, however,
other customs changed. After World War I, downtown businesses started to decorate their interiors and their display windows. Those same stores developed exterior decorations after
the 1930s Depression. At about the same time, the Christmas-
tree presentations in the churches faded, because more and
more families began to decorate individual trees in their homes.

Following World War II, Helena homeowners introduced
decorations to their housefronts and yards. Not until the late
1950s did local civic organizations—and then city government—take responsibility for community decorations. These
changing patterns demonstrate that our ways of celebrating
the holiday season have evolved, and overlapped, and blend-
ed.

The ways in which Helenans mark this special season continue to evolve. During the early 1980s, the community's "Se-
cret Santa" donated hundreds of thousands of dollars to benefit local children, and the program received national
recognition. Many Helenans still cannot conceive of a Christmas season that would not include a performance of Handel's
The Messiah in the Cathedral of St. Helena, or a visit to the
Montana National Guard's "Christmas Dinner at Our House"
in the State Armory, or a slow drive through the Treasure State
addition on Christmas Eve to share the luminarias and the
elaborate light displays.

Because the customs of Christmas do evolve, the celebration of this season is exactly what each of us will make it. It
can be sacred or secular, costly or inexpensive, hectic or con-
templative. For at its core, Christmas offers each of us some
constants: an opportunity to practice "Peace on earth; good
will toward men"; a time to reflect on our past and present
accomplishments and disappointments; a chance to share this
special holiday with our family and friends. And Helenans will

continue to enjoy this glorious, joyous, fulfilling Christmas holiday—just as they have celebrated it for more than 130 years.

HELENA'S
FIRST
HOME PHONES

BY ELLEN BAUMLER

The year was 1876, exactly one decade after the first Western Union telegraph line linked Montana Territory to the "States." Alexander Graham Bell uttered these famous words into his amazing invention, the telephone: "Watson, come here; I want you." Bell no doubt later wished he had said something a little more lofty into the instrument, but nonetheless with those words the world stood poised on the brink of a revolutionary discovery. Bell Telephone Company organized the following year and the telephone quickly captured the imagination of the nation.

Commercial telephone service began in the United States in 1877, two years before Thomas Edison introduced the incandescent electric light bulb to the public. A new railway system stretched from ocean to ocean, and the Brooklyn Bridge was under construction, but in Helena and other out-of-the-way settlements all over the vast continent, there were as of yet no trains. Neither were there electric trolleys, household electricity, nor indoor plumbing. Incredible as it may seem, it was the telephone that preceded all these conveniences. According to the *Anaconda Standard* of January 6, 1907, credit for having the state's first working telephones goes to Helena. For those who collect Helena trivia, this is the story of how the telephone came to town several years ahead of its time.

Professor H.P. Rolfe, a recent graduate of Dartmouth, came to Helena in 1876 with his bride (a daughter of former Governor Sidney Edgerton) to assume the position of superintendent of the public schools. He retained the job for three years before taking up the study of law. Before coming west, Rolfe had spent summer vacations with the U.S. Coast Survey in Vermont, where he had studied telegraphy. He had secured a few telegraph sets, which he brought to Helena. It wasn't long before this hobby captivated two high school students at Central School, James and William Sanders. The Sanders brothers soon had their father, Colonel Wilbur Sanders, also immersed in learning the language of dots and dashes. James, William, Colonel Sanders and Professor Rolfe set about stringing a line between their Ewing Street houses and Central School. The first line extended to the residences of two other nearby neighbors, Governor Samuel Hauser and E.W. Knight: "The line was as crooked as any line of the kind ever strung—being tied to houses and trees." Throughout the summer of '77, the "subscribers" practiced their dots and dashes. All but Colonel Sanders became quite adept at sending messages. Sanders, however, never quite got the hang of it. In fact, he was so clumsy at it that his neighbors begged him to tell them the message ahead of time before attempting to send it.

It was during this summer that the telephone was taking over the East, and the professor obtained a few of the first instruments to cross the Mississippi. He promptly installed them using the telegraph wires already in place. There were no call bells at first. Each subscriber had a code which signaled an incoming call on the telegraph and then conversation could proceed through the telephone transmitters.

The first long-distance transmission was made that summer as well, between Helena and Virginia City. With the help of W.E. Frederick, Helena's Western Union manager, telephones were attached to his company's line. A phone was sent ahead to Father Kelleher in Virginia City. On the appointed day, a veritable concert took place with Father Kelleher singing on one end and Rolfe on the other.

Despite reports of excellent clarity, the poor transmission capability of the 1877 magneto transmitter combined with constant static (which, according to telephone historian John Brooks, was "generally equivalent to that on a modern AM radio during a thunderstorm") called for a kind of "desperate patience." One piece of equipment served as both transmitter and receiver, requiring the user to speak clearly and distinctly

A Helena telephone exchange, around the turn of the 20th century.

into the instrument then quickly transfer it to the ear in anticipation of a garbled reply.

Telephone technology had Helena buzzing with a severe case of "telephonitis." The *Helena Daily Herald* kept its readers apprised of telephone-related news. On February 19, 1878, the *Herald* related the story of a Mr. Jones, who wanted more than anything to possess one of the new instruments: "—his eyes dilated and his bosom heaved with exulting joy as he perused in the *Herald* an account showing how to improvise an instrument—with common twine and a couple of empty oyster cans." Ready to test the gadget, Mr. Jones manned the inside station and sent Mrs. Jones out to "take a snift" at the gate. The couple conversed with the contraption, but the conversation was at times mistakenly interpreted. For example, "of course I can" was heard as "oyster can"; "take care" became "catarrh." Mrs. Jones not only heard her husband's voice coming through loud and clear, but also detected something more: "—an odor, too, seems wafted this way. Haven't you been drinking beer, John?" Mr. Jones denied the accusation and the implication that he had wanted his wife out of the house. This little vignette was apparently meant as a warning of the telephone's less desirable potential.

On February 20, Professor Rolfe hooked up a telephone to Colonel Sanders' Main Street law office via the lines already established at Central School, the Sanders' home and Professor Rolfe's. Experiments with various musical airs, cadences and voices brought great success, proving "the telephonic wonder a practical success." The experiment was also heard by a lady near a telegraph midway between the points of transmission. She reported hearing "voices whistling and laughing and music sent over the wire."

Although the first telephones were leased at the astronomical price of $50 a year, by March, Professor Rolfe was able to borrow locally twenty-two of the instruments for a public Concert and Telephone Exhibition "affording all a chance to test fully this wonder of the 19th century." The event was held at Central School on April 12, 1878. Tickets were sold at various businesses and "family discounts" were offered. Local musical talent donated their skills and songs and speeches were transmitted from remote parts of the city. Proceeds from the event were earmarked for the purchase of "chemical apparatus" for the school. Unfortunately, attendance was only fair and the expense of the event prohibited further demonstrations.

In May the *Herald* reported that the watchtower had been equipped with a telephone connected to the engine house of the Helena Fire Department. Watchman Sam Richardson soon enough had occasion to try out the new instrument by calling in an alarm to the engine house. It proved to be only a burning chimney and the alarm was canceled. All agreed that use of the telephone had prevented sounding the bell and stirring up unnecessary panic.

Helena's lack of a commercial exchange seems not to have impeded the telephone's early use. In lieu of household equipment, makeshift lines were rigged between telegraph offices in different towns. The *Herald* reported one incident concerning a Whitehall gentleman. Just before a severe thunderstorm, he stopped in the local telegraph office and requested use of the telephone to talk with his wife who was visiting in Troy. After finally getting her on the line, he refused to believe it was really his wife on the other end. He asked her to say or do something that might convince him. Just then a tremendous streak of lightning jolted through the wires and knocked the man flat. As he regained his footing he exclaimed, "That's the ole woman, sartin—only she's grode a l-e-e-tle more powerful sence she left home."

The fall of 1878 saw the Sanders brothers and most of their friends off to attend schools in the East. Their home telephones in Helena were put away. The colonel kept his for many years, locked in a curio cabinet. They were the original instruments, all right, stamped with the patent dates of March 7, 1876 and January 30, 1877.

Just a few years later in 1881, Montana's first commercial exchange opened at Miles City. Butte followed within a few months and Helena's exchange opened in May of 1882, a little over a year before the Northern Pacific steamed into town. Rocky Mountain Bell's first Helena directory, published in 1885, listed 148 subscribers and in 1889, when Montana was admitted into the Union, there were 250 subscribers in Helena. The industry was well on its way in Montana, but its path in Helena had already been well paved.

Golfing Amidst Snakes
and Granite

❦

By Leanne Kurtz

A golf club can be used for many things. A threatened home–
owner might wield one against an intruder. A dog owner might
use it to send pine cones or apples or tennis balls skyward for
the pup to chase and bring back, or destroy beyond recognition as dogs will do. A golf club may also be used for its intended purpose—golfing. In the early days of the sport in Helena,
however, golf clubs also became valuable weapons against a
particularly nasty denizen of the sagebrush hills west of town,
the rattlesnake.

While golfing among the greens and decomposed granite
fairways of the Helena Country Club (later to be named Pine
Hills), opened in 1920, patrons kept one eye on the ball and
the other on the ground, ever aware of the possibility that a
rattler may be lurking on the next fairway. No doubt many a
nine iron was pressed into service as a snake killer in those
days. Pine Hills is no longer, but snakes still roam the abandoned course and golfers now enjoy the snake-free links Helena has to offer.

Golf enthusiasts began searching for a place to putt and
drive in Helena around 1915 when T.O. Hammond arrived in
town from Chicago with a collection of "golf sticks." He thought
surely he would find a few courses in the area to practice the
originally Scottish pastime. Finding none, Hammond resolved
to either "get a country club started or sell his sticks, and the
market for sticks in Montana was not very brisk."

Having never owned or used golf sticks, Helenans beset by
rattlesnakes could not possibly have appreciated the value of
this new multipurpose tool. Hammond summoned friends and
acquaintances who he thought would be amenable to learning
the sport of golf, and together they leased Fort Harrison from

the government. The officer's club became the club house and a nine-hole course took shape on the hills overlooking the fort. Helenans now had a brand new recreational opportunity and a gathering place to relive the day's events and tell lies about their low scores and holes-in-one.

War tends to put a damper on fun. When World War I began, golf took a back seat at Fort Harrison to wartime activities, and nobody felt much like playing anyway. When the fort was converted into a hospital, golf enthusiasts had to look elsewhere for a home.

George Lanstrum, one of Hammond's original golfing buddies, first spotted what was to become the new country club and 18-hole golf course west of town, on a site overlooking the "narrow valley of the 'Ten Mile,' and across tree tops to the barren peak of Red Mountain, up above Rimini." The site chosen had formerly been the homestead of Helena's granite-cutting Kain family, and the family's home, made entirely of stone, eventually became a part of the club house.

When the rest of the club house was completed and opened for business in the spring of 1920, it featured two huge fireplaces, baths, locker rooms, and private dining rooms. A front room, which seemed "built of windows," offered club members unobstructed views of the valley and the Continental Divide. The day after the site's grand opening on May 29, 1920, a *Helena Independent* article claimed that "the whole country over knows no more beautiful natural setting than that selected for the new home of the Helena Country Club."

The golfing wasn't bad, either. "The sporty lay of the land," reported the *Helena Independent*, "puts zest into the game, making a careful study of each shot a necessity." The posh club house burned down nearly a year after its auspicious opening. A new club house took its place on the property, but it was not nearly as elaborate. Pine Hills enjoyed substantial popularity among Helenans for twenty years, but war again turned the world's and Helena's attention to other things.

It was about this time that Bill Roberts arrived in Helena by way of Illinois, and Roundup and Billings, Montana. From his days of following golfers around courses in his home state, pestering them until they agreed to let him hit a few balls, to his retirement from the sport in Helena some fifty years later, Bill Roberts was an enthusiastic golf devotee.

Work in the southeastern Montana coal mines as a hosting engineer brought Bill Roberts to Montana in 1913; and in 1927, he established Pine Hill (a popular name!) golf course in Roundup. After serving as the pro at three courses in Billings, Roberts moved to Helena in 1940. He immediately saw great potential in a patch of land on North Benton that Helenans had previously used as an airport. In fact, Charles Lindbergh's *Spirit of St. Louis*, with the "tousle-headed" twenty-five-year-old pilot manning the controls, had touched down on the same gravelly, sagebrush-covered spot during a visit to Helena on September 6, 1927.

With little outside assistance, Roberts tackled turning this dry, rocky piece of land into the nine-hole Last Chance Golf Course. He picked rocks, mowed the weeds and grass, planted greens and fairways, installed a sprinkler system, and built a club house.

As the resident golf pro, Bill Roberts delivered many Helenans into the world of golfing. He particularly enjoyed introducing the sport to kids and has been credited with launching the successful amateur careers of a number of Helena youth.

In the early 1950s, Bill Roberts severely cut his hand on a mower blade. The accident forced him to seriously curtail the sport he had played for most of his life. He remained the golf pro until 1959 when, at seventy-four years old, he retired from full-time golf.

Not quite able to entirely walk away from golf upon his retirement, Roberts agreed to be the caretaker at the links and continued giving hints and tips to anyone who would listen as he tended the greens and fairways. Perhaps even now he is providing inspiration from the Great Beyond to that frustrated golfer (and anyone who has swung a golf stick well knows the frustration of the beginner) slicing into the water, hooking into the window of one of the homes abutting the course, or digging five-inch divots into the turf.

Golf today is not categorized as a life-threatening sport, unless, of course, one chooses to play in a lightning storm, or runs a cart into a pond, or takes careful aim at an opponent who is under par. Helenans enjoying one of the area's three golf course—Bill Roberts, Green Meadow Country Club and Fox Ridge—need not fear bodily injury as Pine Hills enthusiasts did in the 1920s. Golfers these days have a small handful of individuals to thank for bringing golf to the community and providing Helenans with a place to relish the short summer season in a snake-free, decomposed granite-free, airplane-free, sagebrush-free environment.

MORALLY WE ROLL ALONG:
CHAUTAUQUA IN HELENA

BY DAVE WALTER

No institution under the sun takes the place of Chautauqua. For fine fun, for rubbing elbows with one's neighbors away from business cares, for the delight of untangling mental snarls, nothing surpasses Chautauqua. For listening to great religious and political and educational prophets, for hearing unusual music, and for attending worthwhile drama, Chautauqua is matched by nothing else in America.

Ellison-White Chautauqua brochure, 1928

Anticipation began building in Helena long before the Chautauqua train arrived on July 23, 1913. The "advance man" for the Chautauqua company had been in town since late June—coordinating arrangements with local civic leaders and publicizing the week-long extravaganza. Yet it was only when the crew of rugged, well-tanned college men unloaded the mounds of brown canvas from the boxcar that Helenans were convinced that their first-ever Chautauqua would be a reality.

The Chautauqua finally had come to town! It promised to bring solid culture to a community always receptive to this kind of educational interlude. As the "advance man" reflected (Helena *Montana Record-Herald*, August 3, 1913): "The people of Helena are sufficiently interested in the better things of life. And that is proven by their willingness to bring to their community the best thought and the most advanced ideas that the country affords."

Helenans enthusiastically purchased series tickets ($2.00) to the Ellison-White Chautauqua program that ran from July 25 through July 30, 1913. The tent crew erected the canvas theater—fully illuminated by strings of electric light bulbs—

on the tree-shaded grounds of the Broadwater Hotel and Natatorium, "just 15 minutes west of town." Day after day, crowds reaching 1,200 people packed the huge brown tent for morning, afternoon, and evening sessions.

Participants enjoyed a diversity of presentations: from a lecture on Mediterranean society by Julius Caesar Nayphe of Athens, Greece, to interludes by Chicago's renowned White City Band; from concerts by the Thaviu Grand Opera Company to "An Evening of Sorcery" by Harrell, the Boston magician; from musical performances by the Winona Ladies of Indiana to comedy by Marietta LaDell, the Canadian girl humorist; from Ben Chapin's impersonation entitled "Abraham Lincoln Speaks" to a lecture on "The New Woman and the Young Man" by U.S. Senator Elmer J. Burkett of Nebraska.

The highlight of the entire week occurred on Tuesday evening, when the White City Band played a march written by Willie Ericke, the son of Mr. and Mrs. Ernest Ericke of Helena. In fact, Helena's initial Chautauqua experience met with such delight that the Helena Civic Club accepted the responsibility of sponsoring "Chautauqua Week" in subsequent years. That support involved a guarantee to the Ellison-White Chautauqua Company of $1,500 for a seven-day engagement.

A typical Chautauqua tent (in Bozeman), 1928.

MONTANA HISTORICAL SOCIETY

In 1913 the citizens of Helena had received their first taste of a cultural movement that had been spreading across America for more than three decades. The Chautauqua concept emphasized a high level of morality and self-improvement through education and recreation for people of all ages—but particularly for working adults.

Moreover, the Chautauqua movement embodied a definite messianic fervor: these were morally upright people making personal sacrifices to bring knowledge and quality entertainment to a needy audience. That mission of morality derived directly from the founders of "Mother Chautauqua."

In 1874 two long-bearded gentlemen—the Reverend John H. Vincent and Mr. Lewis Miller—conceived an intense summer course of interdenominational study. Both men understood the need to vary the heavy diet of religious studies with current topics, inspirational music, and recreation. They sited the camp on the shore of Lake Chautauqua in western New York State. Well into the 1920s, the term "Chautauqua" represented a spirited movement of self-education that touted the purity of rural life, the importance of community, and the need for every American's social involvement.

During the late 1800s, the Chautauqua movement spread along the East Coast, somewhat into the South, and well into the Midwest. Like the "Mother Chautauqua," these "sister Chautauquas" relied on fixed sites. Then, in 1904, Chautauqua promoters followed the lead of circuit lyceum programs (and circuses) and experimented with a "traveling Chautauqua." The symbol of these "circuit Chautauquas" quickly became the huge brown tent that could hold hundreds of ticket-holders. It was these "tent Chautauquas" that served the people of Montana, beginning in 1910 and running into the early 1930s.

To engage a summer session, community leaders would contact a Chautauqua bureau such as Redpath-Vawter, out of Chicago, or Ellison-White, headquartered in Portland, Oregon. The bureau would book a town when the local committee guaranteed its price (usually from about $750 for a four-day session to over $1,500 for a week-long engagement). The local committee could recoup that guarantee by selling full-session tickets for prices ranging from $2.00 to $3.50 per adult.

The Chautauqua "advance man" arrived at least twenty days prior to the opening of the session. He blanketed the area with advertising, exhorted local committee members to sell more season tickets, and contracted a tent site. Several days before the opening, the Chautauqua superintendent arrived. Remarkable for that era, the superintendent frequently was a woman in her twenties or thirties. Her responsibilities covered all of the session preparations and, once the Chautauqua began, she introduced each act and gave two of the afternoon lectures herself. The superintendent's final, most important duty involved booking guarantors for the next summer's Chautauqua.

The third bureau agent who spent the entire session in town was the Junior Chautauqua director. Young women frequently filled this position too. The Junior director was responsible for all of the children's morning games and activities, for drilling youngsters for a pageant production on the sixth day, and for presenting afternoon story-telling sessions. Often called "the story lady," the Junior director also delivered at least one adult lecture during the week.

Chautauquas frequently charged nothing for a Junior season ticket—but, at most, the week-long pass ran $1.00 per child. In return, each youngster enjoyed a week of education, entertainment, and a costumed role in a Junior Chautauqua production. No wonder Chautauqua left such powerful imprints on an entire generation of small-town children!

During the 1910s, the Ellison-White company dominated the Chautauqua market in Montana and the Northwest. In 1916, for example, the company ran eleven seven-day courses and fourteen five-day sessions in the state. A community the size of Helena could afford the larger version, which included the big-name speakers, musical groups, and entertainment acts. Ultimately, Ellison-White became the largest circuit-Chautauqua on the continent and expanded its presentations to Canada, New Zealand, and Australia.

After Helena's first taste of Chautauqua in 1913, the Helena Civic Club moved the meeting site into town to improve attendance. In 1914 the bronzed college crew erected the huge brown tent on the southeast corner of Ewing and Sixth (the current location of the Retz Funeral Home). For both the 1915 and the 1918 sessions, the tent stood near the corner of Lawrence and Warren, on the athletic field in back of the high school (now the Central School grounds).

In 1915 the Civic Club relinquished control of "Chautauqua week" to the newly-formed Helena Chautauqua Association, which booked the 1916 and 1917 engagements into the municipal Auditorium—a stunning brick building that sat on the northwest corner of Warren and Seventh Avenues. The (Helena) *Montana Record-Herald* (August 8, 1918) explained the move indoors: "Chautauqua in Helena and one good windstorm always go hand-in-hand....In previous years it seems a wind of the Kansas variety has made itself famous by attacking the tent some time during the week of Chautauqua."

During the six summers that Helena offered Chautauqua sessions, the community developed some favorites. The Thaviu Exposition Opera Company, the White City Band from Chicago, and Signor Salvator Ciricillo's twenty-four-piece Italian band always filled the tent. Particularly in 1917 and 1918, bureau lecturers addressed timely topics concerning World War I, ranging from Dr. Frank Bohn's "The Mind of Germany" to Dr. Lincoln Wirt's "Frontline Conditions That I Experienced in France."

The 1918 course offered a special session for Helena homemakers faced with wartime rationing. Mrs. Edith Wilson Roberts shared her secrets on food conservation and provided recipes for "Cottage Cheese Meat Loaf," "Wheatless Yeast Bread," "Corn Meal Gingerbread," and "Cottage Cheese and Liver Salad."

The Junior Chautauqua program also changed annually. The initial 1913 session offered children an opportunity to share activities in the "Ernest Seton Indian Camp." In 1914 the youngsters spent their mornings with William McCormick and his dog "Bronte"—"the mathematical wonder dog, who also has spelled down both boys and girls in action-packed contests." The 1916 session relied on the theme of "King Arthur's Court," and in 1918 Helena children became week-long characters in a "Mother Goose extravaganza." The Chautauqua tradition of providing quality education for the nation's youth certainly played well in Helena.

Despite fervent testimonials and packed tents for some premier events, none of Helena's six Chautauquas generated a profit. Helena's last "Chautauqua week" ran in early August 1918, and that session left guarantors covering a substantial deficit. It became obvious to members of the Helena Chautauqua Association that the Ellison-White lineup offered little variation from what Helenans could find at the Marlow or the Antlers theater on a nightly basis. A solid Ellison-White program still could offer real culture to residents in smaller Montana towns, but both quality music and oration—in addition to moving pictures—were staples in the Capital City.

After World War I, most Chautauqua companies began to modify their uplifting, informative lecture fare by presenting more dramatic troupes and the popular "vaudeville stage acts." This shift from standard educational programming to pure entertainment marked the slow demise of circuit-Chautauqua in Montana and the nation. For instance, by 1921, Ellison-White had stripped its dynamic last-night show of any inspirational lecturers and instead provided a concert by the Royal Hawaiian Quintet, coupled with a presentation of "talking motion pictures" of Hawaii's active volcano, Mount Kilauea.

Ellison-White revenues dropped dramatically in 1922 and again in 1923—despite the company's service to more than 350 towns in the Northwest. In 1925 the bureau abandoned the Chautauqua business completely. Other, low-budget companies moved into the field and served small Montana towns into the early 1930s. The state's last brown circuit-Chautauqua tent was struck in 1932, with the onset of the Great Depression.

The decline of Chautauqua was the result of several other factors, as well as the Depression: the development of radio; automobiles and improved roads, which permitted rural residents to enjoy entertainment in larger towns; the popularity of talking motion pictures; the deteriorating quality of Chautauqua productions. Finally, the national craze for lighter entertainment that rolled out of the 1920s and crashed into the 1930s sealed the fate of circuit-Chautauqua.

Between 1913 and 1918, Helenans shared an important

cultural movement with the rest of America. Here, as in many Montana communities, the long-term effects of Chautauqua remained important and measurable. Scores of memorable Chautauqua performances led children and adults to pursue their interests in music and theater, or prompted them to take up public service, or introduced them to foreign places and topics that they later explored.

Some legacies of the 1874-1932 Chautauqua movement remain. University extension courses, summer sessions, and the vast array of private self-improvement businesses (for example, Weight Watchers, Gamblers Anonymous, and Jane Fonda exercise videos) all can trace their lineage to "Mother Chautauqua."

In addition, book clubs, correspondence courses, and the community programs provided by the Montana Committee for the Humanities and the Montana Arts Council derive from Chautauqua roots. Finally, the entire Elderhostel movement and educational concerns like the Glacier Institute and the Yellowstone Institute owe a similar debt.

For six summers during the 1910s, "Chautauqua week" brought information, inspiration, and entertainment to large crowds of enthusiastic Helenans. Before times changed and technology ravaged the circuit-Chautauqua, Helenans shared an important national cultural phenomenon. One woman who had attended Chautauqua programs as a young child captured that Chautauqua spirit when she said, "It was like a bright light coming into your life once each year." Indeed.

RADON MINES

❧

BY LEANNE KURTZ

If you have any doubts, ask the dog. He would be about sixty years old now (that's 1,000 years to you and me) and is probably still alive. Crippled by old age and arthritis, a fifteen-year-old dog was brought to the Free Enterprise uranium mine near Boulder not long after the mine's medicinal effects had been recognized. Stiff and wobbly, the dog tottered into the tunnel and emerged after a few visits, witnesses swore, romping around like a puppy. Tens of thousands of humans have experienced the same relief from myriad symptoms after visiting one of a number of radon health mines south of Helena in the hills between Boulder and Basin. A uranium mine in the Helena Valley even became a destination for hundreds afflicted with chronic pain. Since the dawn of the nuclear age, people have been flocking to a handful of holes in the ground not to quarry for precious metals, but to breathe deeply the radioactive gasses, seeking relief from painful, debilitating illnesses.

Montana's first commercial uranium ore producer, the Elkhorn Mining Company's Free Enterprise mine began humbly in 1925 as an eight-five-foot shaft dug by hopeful silver-seekers. In 1951, two years after uranium operations had started, a miner from Los Angeles and his wife visited the Free Enterprise. The miner's wife had long suffered from bursitis, but after a few tours of the underground mining operations, she noted that the nagging pain in her shoulder had all but disappeared and she could raise her arms above her head for the first time in years. The woman went home to Los Angeles and shared her experience with a friend, who took her advice, traveled to Montana, and ventured into the tunnels to absorb the healing air. She reported similar results and soon word of the invisible cure-all spread throughout Montana and the country. Within a year, the company's stock had jumped from 50 cents to $2.24 per share on the New York Stock Exchange.

Beset almost overnight by scores of hopeful ailing people and their pets wandering through his mine, Wade Lewis, president of the Elkhorn Mining Company, was careful to avoid publicly extolling the healing powers of the mine. "We are hardrock miners, not doctors," Lewis told the *Independent Record* in a 1952 interview. "We have invited the criticisms of doctors and urge them to carefully examine their patients both before and after visits to the Free Enterprise." Despite the mining company's reluctance to advertise the mine's perceived medicinal benefits, the people kept coming. By 1952, Elkhorn Mining Company officials recognized that as thousands of paying visitors flocked to the mine, their safety and comfort was paramount. Uranium operations were temporarily suspended and the company spent over $100,000 on such improvements as an elevator and seating areas underground as well as a visitor center and waiting lounge above the surface.

The Free Enterprise, the Merry Widow and other radon health mines near Boulder did have some competition in the Helena valley. Following his periodic inspections of the John G Uranium Mine, John Howard would return home and exclaim to his wife who was suffering from the effects of meningitis, "Helen, if you could only get up to the mine, I am sure it would help you. There is something there. I don't know what it is, but it makes me feel as frisky as a colt." When her husband died, Helen Howard took on the strenuous task of cleaning the 900-foot tunnel, installing electric lights and clearing a parking lot. She began the business of healing in 1952, offering use of wheel chairs and charging only what visitors felt they could afford. "…no set price has been made as your relief is the main objective," read the mine brochure.

John G Mine did not have the amenities of the Boulder-area mines, though, and Boulder became something of a "boom town" as the popularity of the radon experience grew. The community of 1,000 permanent residents hosted a new taxi service, modern hotels and railway passenger service to accommodate the mine visitors. "The Diamond S Ranchotel [also known as Boulder Hot Springs Hotel] is bursting at the seams…" reads the caption under a photo in the *Independent Record* showing the view of Boulder from the Free Enterprise waiting room.

Among the breaking local news stories ("Mr. and Mrs. Cass Adair of Auburn, Wash., called on Mr. and Mrs. Warren Hart in Boulder a short time Wednesday afternoon."), the sports scores, and the helpful household hints that made up the *Boulder Monitor* during the 1950s and 1960s were inspirational stories of "miraculous relief" from arthritis as well as asthma attacks, sinusitis, skin conditions, and migraines. Dr. James Wolfe, a physician who visited the Free Enterprise mine in 1956, proclaimed in the *Monitor,* "I have read records of diabetics having left here with no need of insulin...This radon therapy is so new, and the results it gives are so amazing, that actually the possibilities are so great that its ultimate is impossible to visualize."

Other doctors weren't so sure. The Elkhorn Mining Company sought medical and scientific opinions from professionals throughout the United States and Europe. Many could see no scientific reason for the relief the majority of visitors claimed the mine provided. Skeptics believed the radon levels in the mine were so slight, that the beneficial effects were purely psychosomatic. Mining company officials and sufferers of chronic pain, however, could not deny the hundreds of case histories testifying that there was healing magic in that underground air.

While radon gas has been listed as the second-leading cause of lung cancer and the sale of home radon detectors is skyrocketing, most agree that the levels of exposure in the mines are not dangerous. In spite of glowing testimonials from thousands of health mine devotees, the professional medical community remains skeptical about the real benefits of the radon mines. Whether exposure to radon gas is a miracle cure or not remains to be scientifically proven. But on any given day, recreational vehicles from all over the country can be seen parked near the health mines while scores of afflicted humans and, yes, dogs await the relief from pain they are certain the air hundreds of feet below the surface will render.

PLACES

A Place of Singular Appearance?

By Stephenie Ambrose Tubbs

Twenty miles north of Helena lies an impressive canyon whose physical characteristics are familiar to Helenans. Meriwether Lewis described it in his journal entry for July 19, 1805:

> this evening we entered much the most remarkable clifts we have yet seen. these clifts rise from the waters edge on either side perpendicularly to the hight of 1200 feet. every object here wears a dark and gloomy aspect....the river appears to have forced it's way through this immence body of solid rock for the distance of 5 3/4 miles and where it makes it's exit below has thrown on either side vast collumns of rocks mountains high. the river appears to have woarn a passage just the width of it's channel or 150 yds. it is is deep from side to side nor is ther in the 1st 3 miles of this distance a spot...on which a man could rest the soal of his foot....it was late in the evening before I entered this place...obliged to continue my rout untill sometime after dark before I found a place sufficiently large to encamp my small party; at length such an one occurred on the lard. side...from the singular appearance of the place I called it the gates of the rocky mountains...

What is not so familiar to us are the efforts of those who realized this spot and others like it along the Lewis and Clark Trail ought to be memorialized in a way sure to attract the attention of future generations. One such group, the Oro Fino (Helena) Chapter of the Daughters of the American Revolution (D.A.R.), sought to acquire and assume the protection of historic spots, to erect monuments and to encourage historical research.

In 1924, at the state D.A.R. convention in Billings a decision was made to place a bronze marker or two each year until at least the most noteworthy landmarks and sites in the state had been designated. In this pursuit the organization relied upon the "magnificent generosity of Montana's greatest industrial corporation," according to state D.A.R. regent Bessie Elma Rasmusson, "the Anaconda Copper Mining Co. who magnanimously undertook to furnish these markers." The markers, it was to be noted as a source of state pride, were made of native Montana copper and related ores and "are fashioned in a Montana foundry by the ingenuity and handiwork of Montana men." Between 1924 and 1940 the D.A.R. would place thirteen historical markers across Montana.

On July 19, 1927, the 122nd anniversary of the Lewis encampment in the Gates of the Mountains, a festive ceremony dedicating the "handsome tablet" was held at Meriwether picnic ground. The area had been used as landing since 1886, when inaugurated by Judge Nicolas Hilger for his steamboat *Rose of Helena*. Before the D.A.R. monument ceremony renaming it Meriwether, Hilger called the spot "Picnic Canyon."

A crowd of 200 citizens witnessed the dedication, including Judge Hilger's son David in his capacity as state historian, Governor John E. Erickson, Chief Justice Llewellyn L. Callaway, state D.A.R. Regent Mrs. Rasmusson and many D.A.R. chapter members. The marker was formally unveiled by two quaintly dressed children, Fillby Barker and Bobby Smith, who "deposited floral pieces of red, white, and blue at the base of the monument in memory of the explorers." The plaque reads:

In commemoration of the intrepid explorers comprising the Lewis and Clark Expedition who discovered this canyon and encamped here July 19, 1805 on their westward voyage of trans-continental exploration en route up the Missouri River bound for the Pacific Northwest. Dedicated by the Oro Fino chapter Daughters of the American Revolution, July 19, 1927.

In his remarks, quoted in both Helena papers, historian David Hilger stated, "It gives me special pleasure to be invited to accept this gift for all the people of Montana and to express my appreciation of the splendid work of the D.A.R." Hilger went on to do something historians generally try to avoid. He stated that the site being honored that evening was the "exact spot" Meriwether Lewis and his men had camped on the gloomy July night of 1805. According to Hilger, "of the many camps made by the explorers in our state I know of none where the exact location can be more definitely assured than the spot on which these dedication exercises are being held." Hilger commented that the raising of the river by the Montana Power Co.'s Holter Dam in 1918, "had not changed the conditions from that time till now." Hilger arrived at his conclusion after tracing the route of the Lewis and Clark trail by steamboat, by motorboat, by horseback, and by foot. Having compared the maps and the journals, Hilger was convinced that the location was exact as shown "definitely and positively by their records."

Other observers and Lewis and Clark enthusiasts are not so sure. Using the same maps and journals, along with modern tools such as depth finders, these researchers have come to startlingly different conclusions. One such researcher is Butte resident Robert Bergantino, a recognized authority on Lewis and Clark in Montana. He thinks the site of Lewis's camp that night was actually nearly to the mouth of the canyon south of present-day Fields Gulch. His maps, using detailed course comparisons, place Lewis at a site where, in a wet year, gulches would reveal what Lewis describes in his journal as "several fine springs bursting out at water's edge from the interstices of the rocks."

Others wonder why Lewis and his party of some thirty men would not have stopped at Fields Gulch, which would seem to be, as Lewis describes, the first spot in three miles except one of a few yards on which a man could rest the sole of his foot? Bergantino feels the party kept going past Fields Gulch because Lewis believed he could get out of the canyon before nightfall but had to stop when it became too dark.

Robert Lange, former editor of the journal of the Lewis and Clark Heritage Foundation, *We Proceeded On*, states "students of the expedition do not always agree with respect to some locations. However careful study and perseverance rewards researchers with what may be claimed as authentic conclusions." Hilger certainly claimed his conclusion as authentic. Bergantino and other scholars can make similar claims of authenticity. The expedition left little physical evidence behind them so the truth will probably never be known.

What cannot be disputed are the words, if not taken too literally, of Governor Erickson in his acceptance of the tablet on behalf of the state, "Here they rested their weary feet, here they built a fire, here they rested with the dark and solemn river rolling at their feet." Erickson looked forward to the coming years when thousands would journey to the Gates to visualize the meaning of the monument and go away better men and women "with a greater respect and love for their country."

In the spring of 1998, the Forest Service gave Meriwether picnic grounds a facelift and worked to ensure that the lovely site could be enjoyed by everyone. The D.A.R. and the Mann Gulch memorial plaques were moved so that climbing steps to view them would no longer be necessary. The number of visitors Meriwhether receives each year would surely surprise Governor Erickson, as they now total nearly 32,000, not including private boaters. No doubt some of these visitors leave inspired by the scenery and the plaque to do their own Lewis and Clark research just as the D.A.R. intended. An on-site interactive computer kiosk owes its existence to the efforts of Jeff Dobb and the Gates of the Mountains Foundation. Students of the expedition can also find help reaching authentic conclusions by visiting Lewis and Clark at VIAs's world wide web site: http://www.lewisandclark.org.

In the 1920s, before the D.A.R. marker was placed, a sign inaccurately claimed this was the very spot for Lewis and Clark.

MacDonald Pass

BY JON AXLINE

Because of Helena's preeminence as a mining, commercial and political center in the late 19th century, it was by necessity also an important transportation hub for the territory. Besides the Mullan Road and its offshoot, the Benton Road, the Helena–Deer Lodge Road was also an important arterial for the fledgling community. Like other frontier highways, it consisted of little more than a dirt track with many branches and a relatively ill-defined "official" alignment delineated for the benefit of the government surveyors. The Helena–Deer Lodge Road struck out for the Little Blackfoot River Valley via today's U.S. Highway 12 route. About twelve miles west of town, it split into two roads, with one utilizing MacDonald Pass and the other Priest Pass. Although both facilities were toll roads, only one eventually became the primary thoroughfare between Helena, Deer Lodge and other points west.

The first territorial legislature in 1864 authorized the creation of twenty-eight toll road and bridge companies in Montana. In 1869, the legislature re-authorized Constant Guyot to construct a toll road from Helena to the Little Blackfoot River west of Helena. The following year, E.M. "Lige" Dunphy apparently bought out Guyot and completed construction of the ten-mile-long toll road over what would eventually become known as MacDonald Pass. Born in New Brunswick in 1833, Dunphy arrived in Montana with the Fisk Expedition in 1862. For three years he worked for the King & Gillette toll road company before opening his own business in 1865. At the time Dunphy purchased the toll road, he was operating a small sawmill between Helena and Unionville.

When completed, Dunphy's toll road ran from Hartwell's sawmill on Ten Mile Creek to the "Frenchwoman's Ranch" on the west side of the mountain pass. By all accounts the road was in fairly good condition, although it required corduroying in places to carry wagon traffic over the muddy areas. Dunphy also established a ranch and built a tollhouse (which still stands) and gate on the Helena side of the pass.

Shortly after completing the toll road, Dunphy hired Canadian immigrant and sometime prospector Alexander MacDonald to manage and maintain the road while he concentrated on his sawmill business. MacDonald operated the facility for Dunphy until July 1876, when he and John McCrae purchased the ranch, tollgate and road for $2,300. The partners contracted with the stagecoach firm of Gilmer, Salisbury & Company for use of the road. The toll house provided meals to the stagecoach passengers and hay for the horses from a meadow located near today's Cromwell Dixon Campground. In return, MacDonald and McCrae did not charge the stagecoach company for the use of the road. As many as three stages daily traversed the road between Deer Lodge and Helena. The coaches usually carried no more than seven or eight passengers in addition to the mail.

Sometime between 1876 and 1878, MacDonald turned over management of the road to Valentine T. Priest so he could focus on his cattle operation in the Judith Basin. Ownership of the MacDonald Pass Road becomes unclear at this point. Some historical accounts indicate that MacDonald sold the operation to Priest, but there is no record of the transaction in the county Clerk and Recorder's Office. Always looking for opportunities, Priest left the day-to-day operation of the toll road to his daughters while he prospected the surrounding hills. In 1878, he ended his employment with MacDonald and relocated so he could build his own toll road a few miles to the north. With Priest's defection, MacDonald apparently returned to his toll road in 1881 and remained there until he sold it in June 1885. MacDonald relocated to Helena where he worked primarily as an expressman until his death in May 1899 at age fifty-eight.

Use of the MacDonald Pass road apparently declined after Valentine Priest completed construction of his road in 1880. Priest's Pass was 500 feet lower than MacDonald Pass and provided a somewhat shorter route between Helena and Deer

Lodge. An article appearing in the *Helena Independent* also indicates that Priest was able to lure Gilmer, Salisbury & Company away from their agreement with MacDonald. Shortly after 1890, however, both toll roads were acquired by Deer Lodge and Lewis and Clark counties (Powell County was not created until 1901) and they became free public thoroughfares. In 1912, both Deer Lodge and Lewis and Clark counties contracted with the Montana State Prison for the use of convict labor to improve the MacDonald Pass route.

Between 1910 and 1917, when the state terminated the program, prisoners built approximately 500 miles of roads in Montana. Warden Frank Conley believed that manual labor not only restored the convicts' self-esteem, but also taught them a skill they could use upon release. In 1912, nearly fifty percent of the state prison's population was employed in public works projects outside the penitentiary's walls. The convict crews specialized in constructing roads through difficult terrain, such as MacDonald Pass. In return for their on-the-job training, the prisoners were allowed a measure of freedom that was not possible behind bars, and they also could earn a reduction in their sentences—as long as they didn't try to escape. The convict construction camps were generally rather primitive, with the men sleeping in small tents. About seventy-five men composed a work detail supervised by three unarmed guards. The county paid for construction equipment and maintenance of the prisoners if the cost was above fifty cents a day.

Improvement of the MacDonald Pass route in 1912 nearly sealed the fate of Priest's Pass. With the advent of the automobile, the sharp curves and steep grades played havoc with car brakes, rendering the lower elevation and the shorter mileage irrelevant, and traffic on the road subsequently dwindled. Neither pass, however, was included in the state's Federal-Aid highway system in 1914—that honor went to the road that paralleled the Northern Pacific Railroad's tracks over Mullan Pass.

By 1927, MacDonald Pass was included in Montana's federal highway system. In early 1928, the Montana Highway Commission received permission from the Bureau of Public Roads to improve the grade and curves of the treacherous road, and place a twenty-four-foot-wide graveled surface on it. Within months, the Highway Commission had their surveyors on the route mapping the grades and curves. The Nolan Brothers company of Minneapolis won the contract to upgrade the road in early 1931 and construction began on May 18. Because of the Great Depression, the federal government funded all but $810 of the $89,000 project. Federal and state regulations also encouraged the use of local labor, with only a minimum of heavy equipment used on the project. My grandfather, a civil engineer working for the Highway Commission, met his future wife while working on this project. She was the daughter of a local rancher, Harry Adami, who had a ranch at the eastern end of the road at the base of Priest's Pass. Many farmers and ranchers from the Little Blackfoot and Ten Mile Creek valleys were hired by Nolan Brothers to build the road. The firm completed construction of the road in late November 1931. The new road crossed the Continental Divide at 6,325 feet, one of the few spots where the old toll road and the new highway intersected.

In 1935, the Montana Highway Commission further enhanced the road by constructing the first of its section houses just below the Continental Divide. Still in operation, the rustic-style building was intended to provide shelter to men and

The tollhouse, which still stands, and the gate on the Helena side of MacDonald Pass.

MONTANA HISTORICAL SOCIETY

equipment "stationed in storm areas" to keep the pass open in the winter. The water fountains on the pass were improved at about the same time. By 1939, the MacDonald Pass road was described as "highly developed, smooth-surfaced, regularly graded and widely curved...[which] appropriately fits into the scenery and also the economic scheme of things." By 1963, the Montana Department of Highways was planning the eventual reconstruction of the highway to a four-lane facility, a plan that came to pass in 1979.

The tortuous road up to MacDonald Pass has long been an important part of Helena and Montana's history. It was originally one of nearly fifty officially sanctioned toll roads in the territory. While there were many complaints about the condition and fares of the toll roads, they were instrumental in opening Montana to settlement and allowing the import of supplies and industrial equipment and the export of mineral and agricultural products. Unlike most of Montana's toll roads, the history of this road's development to a modern highway is well-documented and a well regarded part of Helena's past. Even today, the winding route up to the pass and down to the Ten Mile Creek and Little Blackfoot valleys is vaguely reminiscent of the ordeal early users of the route must have felt in the 19th century. As a boy in the 1960s, I remember well the white-knuckle terror of my father speeding (or so it felt) down the east side of the pass and the horror of seeing a jack-knifed semi-trailer precariously perched on the shoulder of the road. Even then, the 20th century equivalent of a freight wagon had experienced one of the perils of the narrow, twisting and important road that helped supply Helena in its infancy.

PRIEST'S PASS

BY JON AXLINE

Our frontier forebears were no different from people in the 1990s—always trying to find a better way of getting from here to there. Priest's Pass is a good example. With two good mountain passes west of the city, one man saw an opportunity to add one more route to the growing network of roads that spread across the territory. Valentine Thomas Priest was an opportunist of the classic frontier tradition. Although mistakenly called the county's "first road builder," Priest was, nonetheless, an important figure in the development of Helena because of his faith in the potential of the community. Ultimately, the Priest Pass Road failed to become the main thoroughfare between Helena and points west, but it has since become a favorite backroad for late 20th century recreationalists.

Born in Parishville, New York in 1831, Valentine Priest operated a flour mill in Taylorville, Illinois after marrying fellow New York native Celestia Sanford in 1857. While in Illinois, he contracted tuberculosis and went west to improve his health, as many others did. Priest arrived in Montana in 1864

Priest's tollhouse at the base of the pass near Sweeney Creek.

MONTANA HISTORICAL SOCIETY

via the Bridger Road (the safer alternative to the Bozeman Trail) and spent nearly a year prospecting for gold in the Virginia City area. He returned to Illinois in 1865 and operated a hotel with his brother in Decatur. Four years later, in 1869, Priest, along with his wife and two daughters, Millie and Alice, took the newly completed transcontinental railroad to Corinne, Utah, where they disembarked and traveled north to Montana over the Utah-Montana Road. They settled in Grizzly Gulch near Helena, and Valentine worked for several years as a placer miner, before establishing a sawmill in Colorado Gulch.

By 1878, Alexander MacDonald had hired Priest to manage his toll road. Although local legend states that MacDonald sold the road to Priest, there is no evidence this ever occurred. Instead of taking an active hand in the management of the MacDonald Pass road, however, Priest left the collection of tolls to his daughters while he continued to scour the surrounding hills in search of his Eldorado. Probably in 1879, Priest rediscovered a pass that had been used by prospectors traveling to the Kootenai Country in the early 1860s. Because of the relatively low elevation of the pass (5,984 feet compared to 6,320 feet at MacDonald Pass) and the potential for a somewhat easier grade, Priest terminated his employment with MacDonald with the intention of constructing a toll road over what would become known as Priest's Pass.

Valentine hired Helena civil engineer Benjamin Marsh to survey the new route over the Rocky Mountains. Construction of the road began in late 1879. It took 100 Chinese laborers eight months to construct the road, which was just wide enough to accommodate a stagecoach. The $20,000 road was later described as "coiling like a great serpent up the steep slopes, [adding] another step in the western progress of civilization." Priest built a tollgate and substantial two-story toll house at the base of the pass near Sweeney Creek. From there, Millie and Alice earned $10 a month collecting tolls from sometimes difficult travelers (including a particularly obnoxious character named Calamity Jane).

Evidence also suggests that Priest was able to induce the Gilmer, Salisbury & Company stage line to use his road rather than Alexander MacDonald's route. In an undated article in a

Helena newspaper, the Gilmer, Salisbury Company's Division Agent, Mr. Riddle, praised
Priest's nearly completed thoroughfare as a "good road with
the exception of a few rocks
and a mudhole or two that he
had fixed." The road was so
good, in fact, that usage of the
MacDonald Pass road dropped
sharply, eventually forcing
MacDonald to sell the property in 1885 and relocate to Helena. According to Priest,
Northern Pacific Railroad surveyors even considered using
his road for the railroad's main
line before finally deciding on

Valentine Thomas Priest.

its current course over Mullan Pass in 1882. There is every
indication that Priest's Pass had become the main road over
the Continental Divide near Helena by the time Montana became a state in 1889.

Statehood, however, proved devastating for Valentine Priest
and his road. Because the toll road had never been chartered
by the territorial legislature or by Lewis and Clark and Deer
Lodge counties, it was, in effect, "nationalized" by both counties by 1890 (along with the MacDonald Pass road) and made
into a public facility. Valentine died from Bright's Disease in
January 1890, and his residence, once a social center of the
Ten Mile Creek valley, was abandoned within a few years. By
1939, the dwelling had all but disappeared. Both MacDonald
and Priest's continued to be used by travelers, but most traffic
traversed Mullan Pass even though it was much longer than
either of the roads to the south. By 1914, Priest's Pass road
was in decay and seldom utilized.

The arrival of the automobile in Montana in the early 20th
century briefly injected new life into the aging road. Automobile touring had become an exciting recreational pastime for
many Montanans just before the First World War. Although all

of the state's counties levied road taxes to improve and maintain their roads, the automobile proved no real improvement over the horse in the early 20th century. The counties could not keep up with deteriorating roads that were desperately in need of repair and upgrading. Occasionally, the counties utilized convict road crews to improve roads or, if fortunate enough, the Montana State Highway Commission might be able to improve it through one of their few "demonstration" projects after 1913. Another avenue of road improvement included the many trail associations that flourished in the United States in the years before the World War I.

Before Montana's highways received their numerical designations in 1926, the state's major highways were given names (i.e. the Yellowstone Trail, the Park-to-Park Highway, Buffalo Trail, etc.) and their routes emblazoned with multicolored symbols. Oftentimes, the roads were sponsored by trail associations who promoted them as tourist routes to the nation's national parks. Avid automobilists subscribed to the trail associations with their dues sometimes spent on road improvements. Montana was criss-crossed by at least ten of these auto trails in 1917.

The Priest's Pass road seemed particularly well suited for inclusion in the auto trail system. The pass was over 300 feet lower than MacDonald Pass and the road a shorter route to Deer Lodge and Missoula; it also included the requisite impressive scenery that appealed to tourists. The grades, however, were fairly steep and there were a lot of curves. What seemed particularly attractive about the road to motorists was that it was a relatively well maintained roadway. Consequently, Powell and Lewis and Clark counties likely contracted with the state penitentiary to upgrade the road in 1914. Local rancher Bert Coty supervised the $15,000 project.

In 1915, the road was designated a component of the Great White Way, a series of highways that connected Yellowstone National Park and West Yellowstone with Glacier National Park and Apgar. The route of the road was marked by a white square with a horizontal blue bar. Around 500 people from Powell and Lewis and Clark counties attended the reopening of the Priest's Pass road in late August 1915. Led by a delegation of politicians and good roads activists, a lengthy caravan of automobiles chugged their way up the road and gathered at a meadow at the top of the pass for an "old-fashioned basket lunch." The revelers were treated to a series of speeches, including one by William "Good Roads" Biggs and another by the president of the Montana Automobile Association. The festivities ended with a concert by the Capital City Band.

Reopening the Priest's Pass road as part of the Great White Way was also cause for some extremely gushy prose on the part of the *Helena Daily Independent*. Describing the road as one of the "finest scenic routes" in the West, it eulogized Valentine Priest as daring what even "the railroads had not attempted—cross the Montana Rockies!" and compared him with X. Beidler for his "fearlessness in the extreme." The newspaper also praised the road for its relatively gradual climb, through spectacular scenery, that could be easily accomplished by an automobile in second gear (with only a few places that required it be made in first gear). To accommodate motorists, the counties constructed a series of spring-fed water systems along the road that provided water for overheated radiators.

By 1927, however, the Bureau of Public Roads and Montana Highway Commission designated MacDonald Pass as part of the Federal Aid highway system. While MacDonald Pass was higher in elevation, the grades were less severe and curves not quite so numerous. According to one source, the Priest's Pass road was infamous for its treacherous nature and its propensity for burning out the brakes of automobiles utilizing it.

Today, the Priest's Pass road is administered and maintained by the Helena National Forest. Unlike MacDonald Pass, the alignment of the road has changed little since 1915. The road provides countless recreationalists access to the national forest, with few realizing the history behind this thrilling route across the Continental Divide. It is one of the few roads in the Helena area where one can still experience the excitement of driving a thoroughfare that has not changed since its construction. Like MacDonald Pass, it provided a profound link between Helena and other Montana communities. Interestingly, the proximity of MacDonald Pass to Priest's Pass provides a fascinating contrast between a modern roadway and a remnant from Montana's more rugged past.

East Helena and the Big Fire of 1919

By David Cole

During that same summer of 1864 when the "Four Georgians" were panning for gold in one last chance to hit pay dirt, a wagon train from Iowa was headed for the Oregon country through the Helena Valley. The group stopped along Prickly Pear Creek, near the current site of East Helena, to rest and repair their wagons before crossing the Continental Divide. Among the pioneers were Jonathan and Elmira Manlove and their two small children. They liked the valley land they saw and decided to stay behind and make this their home.

The East Helena Kiwanis Club has relocated the Manloves' original cabin to a site just southeast of the junction of State Highway 518 and U.S. Highway 12 and restored it. According to the Kiwanis, "This is no doubt the oldest structure in the county..." The original cabin site was about one mile northwest of its current location. Part of the East Helena townsite was once the Manloves' potato fields, and their pasture was located near present-day John F. Kennedy Park. Older residents still refer to the tall cottonwoods in the park as Manlove's Grove.

During this period in the development of the Helena Valley, the Prickly Pear House operated as a way station on the stagecoach route between Helena and several gold camps in the Big Belt Mountains. It stood east of Prickly Pear Creek, on the northwest corner of the intersection of Montana Avenue and Main Street in East Helena. The two-story frame structure, which served as a changing point for drivers and horses, provided customers with a bar, dining room, and sleeping accommodations. The Prickly Pear House burned in about 1930.

During the 1870s and the early 1880s, East Helena's current business district was largely cottonwoods and brush.

Following the fire of August 19, 1919, heavy clouds of smoke obscure East Helena's Main Street, where salvaged belongings still await their owners.

Freight wagons frequently camped under the cottonwoods. The Northern Pacific Railroad tracks reached East Helena in 1883, its original station, named Prickly Pear Junction, located near the railroad's crossing of Prickly Pear Creek.

The real impetus for the development of the community of East Helena came from the Helena and Livingston smelter in 1888. Constructed and owned by the Guggenheim investment group of New York, the smelter was to serve the mining industry of the Helena region. The Northern Pacific then extended a spur line through Montana City, up Prickly Pear Creek, to Wickes, Corbin, and Boulder, where it divided. The west leg ran to Basin, while the east leg reached Queen Siding, below the Elkhorn Mining District. Ore from the Marysville Mining District, Granite Butte, Bald Butte, and other areas also fed the smelter operations. The blast furnaces started in 1889 and operated for one year. After a six-month closure, the plant reopened as the United Smelting and Refining Company. The American Smelting and Refining Company (ASARCO) purchased the operation in 1899.

Two families ranching in the East Helena area—the Clarks and the Riggs—subdivided part of their property into a townsite about the same time that the site was purchased for the original smelter. Advertisements in the *Helena Herald* touted the new community: "East Helena is the Place to Invest in Real Estate for Quick Returns."

Real-estate agents for the townsite proposed a railway from Helena to East Helena in hopes that it would spur lot sales and increase land values. By December 1888, the business district already had two general stores, a meat market, and two saloons. Many of the early plant personnel came from the mining camps of Corbin and Wickes, west of Jefferson City, when a portion of the Wickes smelter equipment was moved to the new East Helena smelter in 1888. In 1893, the entire operation of the Wickes smelter was transferred to East Helena.

East Helena was from its beginning a company town. "The plant" provided the primary payroll and the reason for the town's existence, and the company also was deeply involved in community social life. For example, a small lake, created in 1899 by a dam on Prickly Pear Creek southeast of the plant, supplied a cooling water for the smelter. But the same lake furnished the community with boating, fishing, and swimming in the summer and with ice skating in the winter. Named Lake Whitley, after an ASARCO plant manager, it eventually filled with sediment.

The company also sponsored a baseball team—the Smelterites. During the 1920s, this club dominated the Montana Copper League, which included city teams from Anaconda, Butte, and Great Falls. The company often contributed to and subsidized cultural, educational, and civic activities. ASARCO provided a site for a baseball park north of the plant, and in the early 1920s, constructed a nine-hole golf course east of the ball field. During this period, the plant also published a monthly magazine, *The Crucible*, to encourage job safety. It carried news of employees and retired personnel and their families; it also published essays, poems, and articles by ASARCO employees.

The plant's work force tended to be recruited from immigrant populations, and the new community was composed of Austrians, Croatians, Irish, Italians, Montenegrins, Poles, Slovaks, and Slovenians, as well as native-born Americans. At least one half the population was Catholic. The first Catholic mass was held in the Odd Fellows Hall in 1888, seven years before the Sts. Cyril and Methodius Catholic Church was constructed. In 1907, a parochial school was organized. The town also was home to Episcopal and Methodist churches.

East Helena's first school was built in 1890. An 1899 school census found 767 adults (over twenty-one years old), 255 between six and twenty-one, and 228 under six, for a total population of 1,250. Two newspapers competed from 1900 to 1902: the *East Helena Journal* and the *East Helena Record*. They merged briefly and then ceased publication.

Streetcar tracks were extended from Helena during the summer of 1899 and service began in September, making Helena businesses more accessible to local residents. The motormen on the Helena, Hot Springs, and Smelter Railroad developed an informal delivery service for Helena businesses, carrying parcels to East Helena businesses and residents for a minimum charge of fifteen cents. However, even with this improved transportation link, East Helena's business remained predominantly independent and self-contained. A trip to Helena for shopping was considered a special event. A "Smelter" streetcar ran to East Helena from Helena, twice a day, until streetcar service ended in 1927. Nevertheless, most smelter workers lived in the East Helena community itself.

Although East Helena shared damage from the 1935 earthquake with the Capital City and has experienced serious threats from several floods, the most dramatic event in East Helena's development was the disastrous fire of August 19, 1919. In the days preceding the tragedy, Helena's two newspapers—the *Independent* and the *Record-Herald*—carried stories of forest fires in western Montana and of extremely dry conditions posing a severe fire hazard in nearby forests.

The fire was first noticed at 1:00 P.M. in a shed north of Main Street, near Petek's Lane (now Wiley Drive), at the extreme west end of town. It was thought to have been started by children playing with matches or cigarettes over the noon hour. Fanned by a very strong west wind, the fire quickly spread to the east, its intense heat driving back people who tried to fight the flames.

With the smelter whistle sounding the alarm, workers were released to fight the fire and to protect their homes and families. According to one account, "After burning several houses and barns nearby, it sent a spark several blocks into a chicken yard near the big stone house which still stands across from the N.P. depot. [This is the two-story, rubble-stone building known as the "Rock Hut," located near First Street and Pacific—just south of the Cory Dullum VFW Post—which has been used for years by Boy Scout Troop 211.] Flames then blew into the business district."

The extremely strong wind and the lack of a community water system became the nemeses of the firefighters. The *Record-Herald* reported that "Firemen from the East Helena department and citizens are fighting valiantly to stem the fierce flames but are waging a losing battle because of the lack of water and a high wind." At one point, it seemed that the fire's advance could be stopped at the west end of town, but then the wind velocity increased. Burning brands, carried by the wind, leapfrogged the fire line by three blocks.

The *Record-Herald* noted that, "The flames leaped from one building to another, burning with an intense heat that drove the fighters steadily backward. Beginning at the extreme west end of town, the blaze steadily and quickly spread to the east..." According to a local history, "Lacking a city water system, citizens fought with water from wells, mostly hand-pumped, and carried in buckets."

The volunteer fire department, assisted by citizens, used a hand-drawn, one-cylinder pump to draw water from wells, irrigation ditches, and Prickly Pear Creek. The pump worked poorly at the beginning of the fire. Even after its performance improved, its limited capacity was ineffectual against the number of homes and businesses burning simultaneously. About 3:00 P.M., the pump finally broke down during an attempt to save the Richardson Drugstore (which stood on the north side of Main Street, on the current site of the East Helena Volunteer Fire Department station). The engine's connecting rod had snapped, and the machine was left standing in the creek.

The City of Helena sent a fire truck to help, but it proved almost useless without water mains from which to draw. Helena store owners and auto dealers sent trucks to help East Helena businessmen and homeowners evacuate their merchandise and furniture. Smeltermen hauled loads of personal belongings to the smelter, to open fields west of town, and to Manlove's Grove along the creek north of town. Some homeowners could only pile the possessions they were able to rescue in the middle of the street and then watch helplessly as their homes burned. According to a local history by Dr. Stanley R. Davison, "Several merchants moved their stock to the center of the street, where it burned when the heat of fire on both sides set it ablaze."

The fire jumped the slow-flowing creek and set buildings on fire at three locations. The first invasion destroyed the Moreys' White House Hotel on the north side of Main Street, on the east bank of the creek. This might have spread the fire to the east side of town, but fortunately the nearest buildings were a block away and were partially protected by large cottonwood trees.

One of those buildings was the small home of Mrs. Katie Kovich, who was home in bed recuperating from the birth of her youngest son the previous week. As a precaution, smeltermen carried Katie and her child to a neighbor's house two blocks east. The workers also moved her household possessions to Manlove's Grove. For several days, Mrs. Kovich had no idea what had happened to her belongings.

The fire jumped the creek at a second point and burned Peter Hrella's two-story home in the 200 block of Front Street (now Pacific). According to Dr. Davison's history, "The two dwellings next to it were saved only by the determined efforts of their owners, Herbert Plews, Sr., and Joseph Gough, Sr. Armed with garden hoses from a little one-cylinder pump, they stayed on their roofs defying heat and smoke until the blaze next door had died down. Had their houses caught, the fire could hardly have been stopped short of the eastern limits of the town."

The third building burned was three blocks east of the creek: a duplex east of the E.W. Anderson store (formerly the Hrella Brothers' Grocery and now the Little Market) on the southeast corner of Main Street and Montana Avenue. The Hultin family saved their home to the east of the duplex by using a pump and buckets.

The *Record-Herald* reported that thirty houses were burning late that afternoon. The *Independent* said that the rapidly spreading fire was finally halted at the creek and that, by the end of the day, had burned itself out. The next day's *Independent* told its readers that the fire had "...destroyed half of the residence section and practically all of the business district Tuesday afternoon." The Helena papers reported that thirty-four families had lost their homes. Burned buildings and businesses in the East Helena business district included:

U.S. Post Office
H. McGinty grocery store
W.I. Manlove barbershop
East Helena State Bank
I.O.O.F. Hall, above the McGinty/Manlove/bank storefronts
C.P. Callis butcher shop
D.T. Hurd saloon
Kranitz (Kreinitz) residence
Dickey and Barich store
Max Jacob two-story, brick general store
Fraternal Hall above Jacob's store
Hrella and Maronich general store
Gorsich Brothers' meat market
Gorsich Brothers' barbershop
Gorsich Brothers' rooming house
Multz saloon
De Grazia confectionary store and residence
Richardson Drug Company
East Helena fire station and jail
White House Hotel
Maronich saloon

In addition, a number of businesses on Front Street burned, including Kane's Livery Stable (part of the site of the East Helena Volunteer Fireman's Hall) and the Tony Smith Saloon. According to long-time resident Mary A. Smith, all of the buildings on the north side of Front Street from the "Rock Hut" (then being used as a saloon) to the creek were burned. Photographic evidence from Helena newspapers confirms this. A number of saloons catering to smelter workers had stood along Front Street before the fire.

A local history published for the town's seventy-fifth anniversary lists the final results of the fire as "125 people homeless, 45 buildings lost..." Yet reports of the destruction in the Main Street business district differ. The history prepared for the Diamond Jubilee states that the fire burned "...all but two buildings, both made of stone: Flatow's store and the movie house." Davison's history declares that everything was destroyed "...except two stone buildings and two small frame structures between them." The photographic evidence argues that the businesses on the south side of Main Street were completely devastated.

Several local residents who were present during the fire agreed that these four structures survived: the Flatow general store (now the Farside Tavern); a wood-frame saloon to the east (formerly Lucky's Fountain and now a pawn shop); the O'Shea Saloon (formerly the Mint Bar, with its distinctive "1895" keystone archway); and the movie house (now a dental clinic). The former owner of Lucky's Fountain said that the building was saved only because two men stayed on the roof and doused flames with buckets of water.

Remarkably, the 1919 holocaust produced no serious injuries. Further, the community of East Helena recovered quickly. Almost ninety percent of the property owners carried at least some insurance, and most business owners and homeowners rebuilt. Wilbur Manlove, one of seven children of East Helena's pioneer couple, rebuilt his barbershop and continued in business until age ninety.

As the exterior sign notes, the venerable East Helena watering hole, Smith's Place, was established in 1919. The original saloon had been located with the other smeltermen's bars along Front Street. According to Mary A. Smith and Frances Rigler—daughters of the original owner, John J. Smith—their mother insisted that he relocate to Main Street which was considered "nicer." Smith built his new building on the site of the two-story, brick Max Jacobs general store, which was razed by the 1919 fire. Originally the west half of the Smith building was used for the saloon, and the east half was leased to the Shea and Hrella Grocery, and indeed the facade on the east half of the Smith's Place building still retains the "Shea and Hrella's Grocery" lettering.

The City of East Helena incorporated on August 7, 1927, and a community water system was finally installed the following summer. Perhaps more sensitive than most Montana communities to the need for an adequate water system, local citizens supported an $860,000 upgrade of the system in 1988. Almost $2 million of additional improvements are in the planning stage to help deal with East Helena area growth. Not surprisingly, the well-trained and highly-rated local volunteer fire department also receives strong community support.

East Helena's unique history as a cohesive, independent industrial community, its vital function in Montana's mining industry, its cultural and ethnic diversity, as well as its friendly, small-town atmosphere, all contribute to the rich tapestry of the Helena area's heritage. The town's dramatic experience with the fire of August 19, 1919, demonstrates its determination to survive as a distinct community.

NEW CANYON FERRY:
TAMING THE MIGHTY MISSOURI

BY CHERE JIUSTO

*When the historians come around 85 years from now
in the year 2034, they may be looking for evidence of
our prowess in the development of natural assets, including large acreages placed under irrigation by the
new Canyon Ferry dam.*

—Canyon Ferry dedication

On July 23, 1949, eighty-five years after gold was discovered in Last Chance Gulch, a dynamite blast reverberated
through Helena's Missouri River Valley. The blast shook the
original Canyon Ferry Dam to its foundations, and kicked off
construction of a new Canyon Ferry Dam, one that would dwarf
the old hand-hewn stone dam and sentence it to a watery grave.
On hand for four days of festivities were several western gov-
ernors, and Montana's Gary Cooper and George Montgomery.

By Act of Congress, the Missouri River Basin project was
part of a grand plan to place a chokehold on the raging Missouri along its entire length, commandeering its waters for irrigation, hydroelectric power, flood control, and water conservation. Canyon Ferry Dam, a keystone in the upper reaches of
this giant Bureau of Reclamation project, was planned to open
over 500,000 acres of farmland above Fort Benton to new or
improved irrigation.

Similar in design to the Grand Coulee Dam, the new Canyon Ferry dam was an engineering spectacle. Towering 172
feet above the riverbed, the steel and concrete structure
stretched 173 feet across the canyon—large enough to handle
the run-off from over 15,000 square miles of Big Sky country.

It took four years and crews of up to 500 men to string the
enormous concrete apron across the canyon, and erect the

Canyon Ferry Dam towers 172 feet above the riverbed, and handles the runoff from more than 15,000 square miles of Montana.

powerhouse. An old gold dredge was enlisted to excavate the dam footings, and scoop up gravel for the concrete mix. Waste fly ash from industrial stacks was also added to the recipe, to save money and strengthen the bond.

Hampered by shortages of carpenters and a break in the diversion flume, Canyon Constructors rushed through 1950 to raise the dam walls high enough to contain spring runoff. Meanwhile, valley residents scrambled to move or salvage family homes, barns, and other buildings. The Cooney family had the distinction of relocating for a second time; their first move was forced by construction of the original Canyon Ferry Dam across the mouth of Black Rock Canyon in 1898.

Racing ahead of the dam builders, archaeologists from the Smithsonian and Montana State University (Missoula), along with historians from the National Park Service and the Montana Historical Society, combed the floodplain to chronicle the valley's historical legacy before it flooded. They recorded sites, mines, ghost towns, and rock art that told the long story of the Missouri Valley and its people.

The archaeological team discovered cave and rock shelters, and extensive Indian camps, tipi rings, and petroglyphs from the times when the Blackfeet, Gros Ventre and Shoshone regularly occupied this valley.

The historical crew identified remains of human activity from more recent times: three camps believed to be of the Lewis and Clark Expedition, where the door to western expansion was cracked open. Cave Town, Avalanche Creek and other old mining towns, still ringing with the sounds of picks and gold pans from the valley's gold rush days. The Diamond City–Canyon Ferry stage road that wove a loose web along the river corridor, connecting early farms and fledgling towns. And the old rock schoolhouse in Bundy Gulch where children had scratched their futures in chalk on slates.

The Canton ghost town about six miles north of Townsend, included a hotel, dance hall, dry goods store, saloon, bunkhouses, and a homestead that recalled a bustling past:

> As many as 108 couples at one time [danced] on the floor at Canton...It was a gathering place or community centre for the people of the valley. There they came for letters from their friends back home. There the women bought their groceries and dry goods. On Sundays, the young men gathered to run foot races, to play poker and see horse races. Gambling was wide open everywhere. But horse racing was the favorite sport and Canton held no mean record as a racing center, some of the pony races run on her lane were as good as could have been seen anywhere in the state.

All this and more lay in the path of the new Canyon Ferry reservoir, which swamped twenty-five miles of river bottom, and overran the banks of Lake Sewell, the reservoir created by the first dam. When the spillway gates were shut in September of 1953, 2 million gallons—fifty times more water than Lake Sewell—backed up to form Canyon Ferry Lake.

The lake took two years to fill. Four more years passed

before the Helena Irrigation Project—a two-and-a-half-mile tunnel snaking under the Spokane Hills, the thirty-two-mile Helena Irrigation Ditch, and the Lake Helena regulating reservoir—was finished. On April 1, 1959, the taps were opened and water from Canyon Ferry flowed out to irrigate Helena-area farms.

Above the dam, Canyon Ferry village remains today. A cluster of small houses at the head of the reservoir (now used by Canyon Ferry Limnological Institute), it was home to the dam engineers and builders. The heart of the village is the old Canyon Ferry Schoolhouse, built about 1916. While the old ferry landing and townsite lie 170 feet down at the bottom of the lake, the schoolhouse was moved up to the village before the waters rose, and saved. Today it remains...a place to visit, a place to remember, and a sturdy link in the long and eventful chain of Black Rock Canyon history.

BUILDINGS

THE HELENA
ASSAY OFFICE

BY HARRIETT C. MELOY

Helena miners, businessmen and politicians pleaded for the establishment of a mint in their city long before the 1874 Congressional decision was made to build the next best thing—an assay office. Robert Fisk, *Helena Weekly Herald* editor, in April 1868, addressed himself to one phase of the problem: "Obvious and urgent is the need for a branch mint since the establishment of a mint in Helena will swell the metallic circulating medium of the nation at least millions annually."

Helena's first public building, the assay office, a gift from the federal government, was constructed in the Vawter Block, virtually the center of the city, in 1875. The purpose of the new office was to analyze precious metals found in ore bodies and to separate them from the host material by a complicated fire method process. Because this necessary procedure could now be offered in Helena, miners were saved much time and trouble because their gold could be converted into bullion and deposited in their own bank. Previously, gold was sent to Philadelphia, St. Louis or another urban center at great expense to the sender, who waited months before knowing that his gold arrived and what its value was. Small wonder there was dancing in Helena's streets when passage of the 1874 Congressional Act was announced.

A $75,000 building was erected on land purchased from C.L. Vawter immediately after receipt of the good news. At least three men were credited with architectural planning of the red brick structure. The design was similar to many buildings of the day, a typical example of Italianate architecture—arched windows, granite corners and a mansard roof. Reliable sources reported that A.B. Mullett, supervising architect of the U.S. Treasury Department, might have stopped off in Helena

An early photograph of the Assay Office on Broadway.

after completing construction of the Pioneer post office in Portland in 1875, and had drawn plans for the new building. Mullett was only in Helena briefly when William Appleton Potter was named "Supervising Architect" in January 1875. Potter, the son of the Bishop of Pennsylvania, Alonzo Potter, was said to be extremely able to take the place of the celebrated Mullett.

One newspaper account confidently maintained that Frank Michael Meyendorff designed and built the Assay Office. "Mike" as he was called by a host of Helena friends, was the son of a Polish nobleman. He and an older brother had taken up arms against the Russians in their country's fight for freedom. Because of the insurrection, Mike and his brother were banished to Siberia. The brother escaped and fled to America where he, equipped with a fine military training, became a member of General William T. Sherman's staff.

Through Sherman's influence, Mike was brought to America with the understanding he would never again return to Poland. After earning a degree from the University of Michigan, he came to Montana where "he designed and built the building that stands on the corner of Broadway and Warren today." Meyendorff became the first melter when Russell Harrison, son of Benjamin Harrison, became the first assayer. It should be mentioned that the position of assayer was considered "choicest of political plums that any Montana politician could receive." Meyendorff lost his position as melter after Democrat Grover Cleveland was inaugurated president for his second term. The Pole lived in Helena until 1895, for two years a resident in Lenox at 1815 Jerome. This popular son of Poland left Helena to expose land frauds for the federal government in Utah and Colorado. He died in Portland in 1908.

We may never know the true architect of the government building, but we do know that most residents were highly pleased to provide a home for this very necessary and desirable establishment on the prominent street of Broadway.

The building was always described as substantial and dignified, but never as beautiful. One Helenan commented in the *Helena Weekly Independent* of September 6, 1883, about the "want of taste displayed in the architectural structure of the building." He mentioned further, "Uncle Sam has constructed a great many buildings, east, west, north and south, but the assay office in Helena is the only one of the many we have seen which does not make some show of good taste in its structure." Evidently the critic found Richardson Romanesque or Eastlake styles used for homes and public buildings in the late 1870s and early '80s more to his taste.

Assayers, the chief managers of the office, appreciated the equipment and machinery available in the building, and the professional staff. Evidently, though, assayers came and went according to the whim of the seated U.S. President.

One well known Helena-based assayer was Benjamin H. Tatem, named by Republican president William McKinley and retained by McKinley's successor, Theodore Roosevelt. Tatem came to Helena in the late 1860s, and attained success as a miner for several decades. He was actively engaged in mining at Park City, Unionville and Marysville. For a few years he built and managed the Helena Iron Works in a building at "164 W. Main." The family residence was on the second floor of the unusual Italianate style structure. This building, which still exists, housed a number of businesses over the years. The address since has changed to 440 South Park.

Tatem served as chief of the assay office for eight years. One of his other noteworthy activities was founding the Montana Fair Association on whose board he served until the State of Montana assumed control of the summer event.

His home at 529 Floweree, one of Helena's "most elegant west side homes," was built in 1890. Tatem himself was highly esteemed in his adopted home town. At his funeral in 1915, it was said that his many good deeds "were known only to himself."

Vast amounts of bullion were processed at the building at 206 Broadway. One news article reported that $70 million passed through the U.S. assay office from 1876 until 1934, when the office closed.

Owned by Mrs. Wanda Christofferson, the building retains its original external appearance. Helenans are pleased that this vestige of our gold mining era stands as a reminder of a rich and romantic history.

The Bluestone House

❦

By Ellen Baumler

Sometimes Helena does not give up her secrets easily. Sometimes she does not give them up at all. Consider the Bluestone House, perched silently atop its hill for more than a century. The legends about this magnificent Victorian-era monument are familiar to anyone even remotely interested in the history of our town. Most Helenans will tell you that architect James F. Stranahan built the beautiful home for his bride, Leona, in 1889 and that he died leaving it unfinished, his widow bereft. Some might remember the Bluestone House as the family home of James F. McIntosh, while others will swear that the place was once a house of ill repute. It has also long been an accepted fact that the 1935 earthquakes left the building uninhabitable. The truth is that these may not be the facts. The written record, however, has its own mysteries that are as intriguing as these oral traditions.

D.A. Bentley filed the first title for this land with the probate judge in 1869. Ownership passed to E.M. Dunphy in 1871 and to Josephine "Chicago Joe" Airey in 1879. By the 1880s, she, along with other up-and-coming Helena madams Belle Crafton (who later took the name Mollie Byrnes) and Lillie McGraw, owned considerable property in the immediate neighborhood. In 1883, the same year that she built her notorious establishment on the corner of Joliet and Wood streets, Lillie acquired title to this lot which adjoined and lay behind her business properties. On September 9, 1889, Leona Smith Stranahan acquired the title from Lillie but less than three months later, on November 30, Leona passed the title to J.S.M. Neill. James Stranahan, the acknowledged builder of the Bluestone House, never figures in any of these transactions. If he did build the house, for whom did he really build it?

According to the *Record Herald* of January 1, 1889, James Stranahan had practiced in New York and Minneapolis and was a junior member in partnership with local architect Fisk J. Shaffer. Stranahan resided at 123 Jefferson during the apparently brief time he spent in Helena. It is unclear when he married Leona Smith, but according to the federal census of 1900, she was widowed after one year of marriage. Their child, a daughter named Grace, was born in

The Bluestone House has had many owners, almost none of whom lived here.

November of 1889—the same month that Leona sold the property, and perhaps the unfinished Bluestone House, to Neill.

Leona was the daughter of Alexander B. and Corinda Smith. Alexander was a Helena policeman and later night watchman at the assay office. Her brother, Rae Q. Smith, may be remembered as chief deputy in the clerk and recorder's office. It has been said that Leona went to live in the East after Stranahan's death. In fact, she and Grace lived with Alexander and Corinda from 1893 until well after the turn of the century. Leona briefly moved to Butte in 1908 but returned in 1911 and remained with her family in Helena until at least 1920. Records fail to disclose what happened to her after that, or what became of Grace.

An 1890 Sanborn insurance map of Helena clearly shows the Bluestone House still under construction and a second map shows the dwelling completed in 1892. Who completed it? A steep stairway descends from the hillside to Joliet Street where Lillie McGraw's large establishment (two buildings connected by a covered walkway at 34 Wood Street) extended along the west side of Joliet. Even so, nothing indicates that the Bluestone House was anything other than a private dwelling. It is clearly marked as such, even though "female boarding houses," the nineteenth century euphemism for brothel and so labeled on the map, are its closest neighbors. Indeed, by 1892, the property owner was artist Ralph DeCamp, whose landscapes would later adorn the state capitol. At this time DeCamp was a respectable partner in the Helena Abstract Company and himself newly married. Although DeCamp owned the home until 1896, according to city directories he never lived in the house nor did he use it as a studio.

Paula Petrik, author of *No Step Backward* and the foremost authority on Helena's red-light district, adamantly maintains that there is no connection between the Bluestone House and Wood Street businesses. She would argue that the curious placement of the house is largely due to Stranahan's eccentricity. After all, the Catholic church was party to the same strange juxtaposition, building its St. Aloysius Select Boys School (now Immaculata Hall) in such a way that classrooms overlooked Wood Street activities. It seems a reasonable theory, however, that Stranahan likely built the Bluestone House as a private residence, perhaps for Lillie McGraw, who was making tidy sums of money in her Wood Street business. Her contemporary, Mollie Byrnes, had a beautiful new home a few blocks away at 212 State. Perhaps Lillie overextended her finances—records do show she mortgaged her other property at about this time—and could not afford to complete the home. The intended resident, however, remains in question.

Continuing the trail of ownership, the property passed from Ralph DeCamp to Louis Curtin in 1896 and through a number of different owners until James McIntosh bought it in 1924. Interestingly, no record could be found of any owner ever living in the house. No census exists for 1890, but records for 1900, 1910 and 1920 never reveal any tenants in the building, or at any corresponding Wood or Joliet Street address.

The McIntoshes are almost always cited as having lived in the Bluestone House. This misconception stems from the fact that the McIntosh home had a street address of 80 S. Warren, which is the present address of the Bluestone House. The family long owned the property, but apparently never lived in the Bluestone House. When Emma McIntosh died in 1953, her obituary noted that she had lived at 80 S. Warren "since she came there as a bride 62 years ago." Maps of 1927, 1930 and 1953 clearly show that the Bluestone House was not located at 80 S. Warren but rather at $34\frac{1}{2}$ Wood Street. It was only after the McIntosh home was demolished that the Bluestone House received its present 80 S. Warren address.

The physical appearance of the building has also led to its misidentification. Mollie Byrnes' lucrative business at Joliet and State, diagonally opposite Lillie McGraw's, was called The Castle. The Bluestone House, by virtue of its prominent location and fortress-like appearance, did in truth look more like a castle than Mollie's place did. Al Gaskill notes on April 5, 1964, in his popular 1960s *Independent-Record* column, "The Man in the Brown Derby," that Chet Huntley did the Bluestone House a disservice in perpetuating one of Helena's deep-seated myths by misidentifying it as The Castle during a local centennial celebration. Gaskill relates that the McIntoshes' daughter (coincidentally also named Leona) was quite upset at the association, but Gaskill then creates his own piece of the legend in stating that both Earl Mellon and Bill Flesher owned the Bluestone House and lived in it before the McIntoshes. Neither of these appear in the title transfers; they are not listed in the federal census nor in the city directories. Gaskill also maintains that the Bluestone House had an address of 304 Joliet. A Joliet Street number is possible, but it clearly would have been in the 0-100 block.

Finally, what of the earthquakes? While the Bluestone House was further damaged by the earthquakes, it had been uninhabited long before 1935. There is a maddening gap between 1892 and the next Sanborn map, which does not appear until 1927. The latter, however, shows the house as already vacant as do the maps of 1930 and 1953. However, Vera McIntosh, James and Emma's daughter-in-law, says that she and her husband did live in the Bluestone house in 1940 and 1941. She also insists that Emma's parents lived there at some point before the 1940s. No written record, however, could be discovered of either occupancy.

The 1970s saw the Bluestone House miraculously reconstructed with grant monies obtained by the Urban Renewal Historic Preservation Committee. Additional federal funding was allocated in 1983. The restoration was carried out by dismantling and numbering each stone, then putting the building back together again, one granite block at a time. Its resurrection was like recovering a long-lost jewel in the Queen City's crown, but this architectural treasure is also a true enigma. We may never know for whom it was intended or what early residents—if any—enjoyed the sweeping view from its copper-clad dome. Perhaps that is just as well since the mystery adds greatly to its special appeal.

Hearty thanks to Bill, Rita and Russell Gowen of Helena Abstract and Title Company for allowing me access to title information. Special thanks to Bill, who generously took the time to help.

St. Joseph's: A Haven for Children

By Vivian A. Paladin

In 1869, only five years after gold was discovered in Last Chance Gulch, a group of five dedicated women arrived in Helena by stagecoach with an awesome mission: to educate and guide young adults, to serve the sick, the insane, and the growing numbers of children left without care, often as the result of the death of one or both of their parents.

They were Sisters of Charity of Leavenworth, Kansas, whose compassionate presence in Helena and the Helena Valley spanned nearly a century. A scant year after their arrival in 1869, the Sisters established St. John's Hospital on South Ewing. It was the first of many institutions, housed in a succession of buildings, that would occupy what became known as Catholic Hill.

At St. John's they cared not only for the physically ill, but until 1881 for the mentally ill as well. The latter patients were housed in a small building in back of the main hospital. When the territorial legislature awarded the contract for care of the insane to a private partnership in Warm Springs, the Sisters almost immediately found a new and desperately needed use for the vacant little building on the hospital grounds.

Sister Mary Baptist Carney, administrator of St. John's at the time, was asked to accept and care for three motherless brothers from Butte. "This is an opening for the use of the vacant building," Sister Mary Baptist was quoted as saying, "and I believe the Lord intended us to get into this work."

The Sisters cleaned and refurnished the building and renamed it St. Ambrose's Orphans Home for Ambrose Sullivan, the oldest of the brothers, all of whom would spend their youth in the care of the Sisters and would distinguish themselves later in life. Both Ambrose and his brother, Stephen, entered the priesthood, while their younger sibling became a physician, practicing for many years in New York City.

The Sullivan boys were soon joined by many other children whose parents were either deceased or unable to care for them. By the end of the first year at St. Ambrose's, there were eighteen more children, and still they kept coming until there were forty and dozens of others had to be turned away. It was obvious the little building on the grounds of St. John's could no longer hold them.

In 1890, Mother Josephine Cantwell, once Superior at the Mother House in Leavenworth, Kansas, and now Superior at St. John's, launched her determined campaign to acquire land and build a facility for the care of children in the Prickly Pear Valley just north of the city limits.

On the northeast corner of North Montana and Custer Avenue, on land now occupied by ShopKo, Albertson's and other businesses and their adjacent parking lots, a substantial brick building emerged in a little over three years. The *Weekly Herald* of Helena, in its issue of September 14, 1893, reported on the successful completion of the building in spite of the financial panic then gripping the country.

"To Mother Josephine of St. John's Hospital is due the credit for originating the project, which, with the help of the good people of Helena, and other Montana cities, she has pushed to successful completion in spite of the hard times," the paper said. "The building, which will be ready for occupancy in about two weeks, is one of the finest structures in the State...It is a three-story brick, standing on a high foundation of blue stone. It fronts the west and is 100 feet long north and south and 80 feet wide east and west." Thanks to the generosity of suppliers of materials and labor, low interest, long-term loans granted by local bankers, and donations of everything from shade trees to iron bedsteads and bedding, the cost was kept in the $35,000 range. The home was dedicated on October 8, 1893, with U.S. Senator Thomas H. Carter delivering the address of the day.

From the beginning, there were no ethnic or religious priorities for acceptance at St. Joseph's. The criterion was need. The mission was to see that the children were well dressed, well fed, trained to perform useful work, and well grounded in basic education.

From all accounts, most of the boys and girls were healthy, well-adjusted and happy, although as a reporter for the *Montana Daily Record* of Helena wrote in a long article published on October 5, 1903, there were sometimes signs of sadness. "Some pairs of big eyes turned to the visitor contain an appeal in them for the mother or the father from whom they were lately separated," the article said, "but time and kindness cures all that and eventually these unfortunate little waifs will enjoy life with the vast majority of the merry children about them."

The main theme of the long *Record* article was, however, the need for expansion. In 1903, the original building was bursting at the seams, housing 214 children in a facility designed for no more than 175.

"The children are placed so close together at the dinner table that there isn't room for their cups beside their plates and they are packed on the benches like peas in a pod," the newspaper reported. "The beds in the girls' dormitory are placed so close together that the children can with difficulty edge their way between them."

On the northeast corner of North Montana and Custer Avenue, the substantial St. Joseph's emerged between 1890 and 1893.

By this time, another administrator with formidable credentials had taken charge at St. Joseph's. She was Sister Rose Vincent, who had been a member of her order for nearly thirty years and had spent twenty-two of them in Montana.

"For many years Sister Rose Vincent taught in St. Aloysius School for Boys in Helena," the *Record* said in its article. "Perhaps that is why she has never had any trouble with them. 'Whip them?' she said in reply to a query. 'It is very rare indeed that we find it necessary to punish any boy. Contrary to the belief held by many, boys are not naturally bad. Through associations boys become bad; through associations they become good'."

It was under the leadership of this wise and good woman that the critical expansion work at St. Joseph's took place. With the remaining $20,000 construction debt paid off, new buildings rose on the grounds which by now had grown to ninety-nine acres from the modest three and a half acres first acquired by Mother Josephine.

Expansion work eventually resulted in additional dormitory space, a three-story schoolhouse, separate buildings containing a laundry, a bakery, and a spacious barn for the dairy herd. There was a large vegetable garden, even an outdoor swimming pool. And there was room for 225 children.

There was never a time when the Sisters of Charity failed to receive full community support for their work. Women of Helena regularly met to sew for the children, their work consisting mainly of refitting and making over used donated clothing. The annual fall Turkey Shoot under direction of the men of Helena was a major fund raiser for many years.

Shoes were the biggest item in the clothing budget, it was reported in 1903, although the Sisters were able to buy them in large lots and didn't worry too much about sizes, for "there was always someone who could use them." Good management and a generous community kept costs amazingly low, a far cry from today's institutional costs. In 1903, the monthly cost per child at St. Joseph's was $7.61.

Inevitably, changes began occurring in the Helena Valley. Extensive irrigation projects made possible by hydroelectric plants on the Missouri were making croplands increasingly productive. There were new water recreation facilities and burgeoning housing, and state-of-the-art dredging equipment was extracting gold from the Valley's gravels directly across North Montana Avenue from St. Joseph's.

More importantly, for this and other private institutions dedicated to the care of children, social and medical advances gradually diminished their need. Fewer mothers were dying in childbirth, and public agencies were taking over a greater share of care for needy children.

In October 1935, a series of deadly earthquakes struck Helena and particularly the Helena Valley, severely damaging the complex that had nurtured so many children for so long. The nearly 300 boys and girls were first moved to various locations around Helena, including passenger cars provided by the Northern Pacific Railroad, cars that also doubled as classrooms for high school students whose new building became an earthquake casualty. It was not long before St. Joseph's children, through the influence of U.S. Senator James E. Murray, were moved to the spacious Boulder Hot Springs resort.

Repairs to St. Joseph's, completed in 1937, allowed the children to return. The Sisters soon realized, however, that the need for their home was diminishing. As the 1940s approached, the school on the grounds was closed, and the remaining children began going to school in Helena by bus.

In 1959, just as the Sisters determined to close the doors of St. Joseph's, Fidel Castro came to power in Cuba. Alarmed Cuban families sent their children in large numbers to this country for refuge, especially to Catholic institutions designed to care for children.

For several years in the early 1960s, then, the halls at St. Joseph's again rang with the sounds of youth, this time with a Spanish accent. There was Latin music and "fractured English" as the young Cubans were cared for by the white-clad "Seestaires" who were trying hard to learn the language of their new charges.

By the summer of 1965, residents at the home dwindled as more and more of the Cuban youngsters were reunited with their families. It was then that Bishop Raymond Hunthausen, in concert with Mother Leo Frances Ryan of the Sisters of

Charity in Leavenworth, decided to close the doors of St. Joseph's forever.

The land was sold to the Montana Power Company, and eventually the buildings were demolished and the land cleared of its aging trees. There was talk in the late 1970s that a shopping center to be known as Frontier Mall was planned, but official moratoriums on such developments effectively stopped any such plans.

In 1987, veteran miner Al Ballard and his family, in association with Butte mining interests, opened a placer mining operation at the site, sluicing gravel native to the area and later trucking in ore from Grizzly Gulch. Although criticized in some quarters for their gravel-hauling activity and for despoiling these historic grounds, Ballard and his associates could point to the fact that their operation, which ended in 1990, had effectively filled in much of a swamp-like area on the eastern edge of the property with the gravel they had worked.

When their St. Joseph's Home for Children closed in 1965, the Sisters of Charity of Leavenworth went on to other assignments. But their presence in Helena and the Helena Valley in appreciable numbers and in the full habit of their order is still felt and remembered.

When one considers the contributions these valiant women made to the welfare of children, it is important to go back once more to 1903 and the *Montana Daily Record*. In a statement that still resonates today, the reporter wrote, "The condition of these children is infinitely better than many children who have homes of their own, and who yet know the meaning of neglect and want."

THE IRON FRONT BUILDING

BY HARRIETT C. MELOY

The Iron Front Hotel, one of the most distinctive 19th century buildings in Helena, was unique in this region when it was built—and this is as true today as it was on opening day in 1888.

Iron front buildings in New York and Boston became extremely popular soon after they were invented and introduced by James Bogardus in 1848. Bogardus intended the iron structures to look like stone, imitating Italian Renaissance palaces. But he learned to respect even more the advantage of building with iron because the pieces were not as heavy to work with as beams of lumber, and more impressive—the iron lattice construction of the facade allowed more light to show into the building's interior. The invention was actually a precursor of the 20th century skyscraper.

Margot Gayle, chair of Friends of Cast Iron Architecture and president of the Fine Arts Federation of New York, wrote this in a 1975 issue of *Historic Preservation*:

Iron fronts for buildings were prefabricated at a foundry in hundreds of separate pieces large and small (as large as a column, as small as a rosette). These were molded, polished for fit before being brought to the building site where they were bolted together like parts of an erector set and attached to a building that has been constructed to receive them. The building would have brick rear and side walls, and wooden floors resting on wooden beams and joists. While the self-supporting iron front was a breathtaking novelty, the building behind it was a conventional brick and wood construction.

The building advantages of cast iron attracted venturesome developers of Helena in 1888-1889, when population was booming and housing was scarce. Among such men were Porter,

Muth and Cox, who had earlier platted and developed residential areas around town. In 1888, they jointly purchased a three-story building on North Main called the Windsor House. Commissioning architects Heinlein and Mathais, the group built a four story hotel on the site.

The architects met with Jonathan Stedman, who owned an iron foundry and was eager to supply pieces for the unusual building. When construction began, the original three story hotel was subsumed by the larger building and in fact, gave its name to the new hotel. It seems, however, that the building's distinctive architecture suggested a companion name: the Iron Front Hotel.

Always a popular accommodation on North Main, the Windsor House was even more in demand when the Great Northern Depot, three blocks away, helped to unload passengers to a welcoming Helena in 1909. At that time there were sixty-two elegant guest rooms in the hotel that rented for $1.50 to $2.00. As in European hotels, the bathrooms were off the hallway rather than in each room. An elevator delivered patrons to each floor, and a restaurant just off the lobby served them. The new Windsor House hotel served to anchor the character of Main Street's north end, a role the hotel still plays today. To add a further touch of distinction to the building, "the House Republican members of the First Montana State Legislature regularly convened in the fourth floor meeting rooms."

In 1920, the Independent Order of Odd Fellows and their sister lodge, the Rebekahs, purchased the hotel for $30,000 and remodelled it with another $50,000, and changed its name to the Templeton Hotel, a name which stuck until the name Iron Front Hotel was restored in the 1970s. Both groups—the I.O.O.F. boasting of more than 400 members, and the Rebekahs at 226 members—were exceptionally proud of one aspect of the remodelling: the addition of a ballroom on the 4th floor, a ballroom with large springs under the original oak floor that improved the pleasure of dancing. It's been said that people came from miles around to test the floor.

In 1924, at a Leap Year Dance, the Beveridges' orchestra played. A profit of $49, after expenses, was made from the $100.25 worth of tickets sold. Isaac Miller, who hailed from

Pennsylvania, wrote to his faraway family telling them of his enjoyment of dancing in Helena. A collection of dance programs he kept for years attested to the time he spent at the I.O.O.F. hall. He reminded his family that he was a member of the Republican Party and the Independent Order of Odd Fellows and that even at the age of eighty-five, he was still painting and dancing.

A number of managers presided over the hotel beginning with P.A. Gingereau in 1890; Mrs. Carrie Reed in 1901-02; in 1910 Mrs. Kittie Farady was proprietor; in 1925 Sarah Spencer and Frank Haskins were managers; in 1939-40 Mrs. Phoebe Baynham presided over the front desk; John Morgan checked in customers in 1983-84.

During the early 1970s a variety of young merchants began to occupy the Iron Front shop areas along the Gulch. Ray Domer was the first to try his luck at merchandising in the soon-to-grow complex. He called his business the General Mercantile, which describes his collection of plants, pottery, soap, wooden utensils and coffee grinders.

Pete Peterson, proprietor of the opera House sold records, Joe Estenson found space for his Brew House and record shop; Carly Radley sold clothes from Carly's Closet. Bert and Ernie's Last Chance Saloon & Deli (Tom McCarvel and Tim Kennedy) offered Reuben sandwiches and beer to standing-room only crowds. The *Independent Record* called them "the new breed of merchants" and wished them success. Today, Petrotech offices from Texas are occupying space on the first floor.

In 1972 Nelson and Eve Seeley purchased the building and restored its earlier name. They may have had an inkling of the complexity of the task in restoring the old Iron Front building, but only they know of the grinding work and long hours that went into the improvement and repair of the hotel. Nelson's description of improving and painting the entire facade is a story all of its own. Friends of Cast Iron Architecture honored Nelson L. Seeley in October 1981, by awarding him one of only seven citations given in the country for his work in rehabilitation of the significant cast iron building. His was the only property west of the Mississippi so honored.

EVENTS

One Dark, Cold February Night

By Marcella Walter

The scene will be familiar to many Helena residents: it's a desperately cold February night; a railroad crew on the east slope of Mullan Pass argues over how to handle their train in the icy black; before anyone knows what is happening, cars are out of control, careening east toward Helena and to an inevitable crash.

Many Helenans would pin this scene to the early morning of February 2, 1989, and identify it correctly as the crash of Montana Rail Link (MRL) train #121. They would call it the prelude to an explosion that cut Helena's electrical power for six hours in sub-zero temperatures, damaged all of Carroll College's buildings, and triggered the evacuation of 3,500 Helenans from their homes.

But this dramatic sequence also defines the night of February 15, 1900, when Northern Pacific (NP) freight #54's locomotive pitched off the tracks west of Helena, above Birdseye. It dropped 200 feet into snow, while its cars splintered on the tracks above.

For Helenans who find every February a fight for sun, warmth, and relief from ice, these two train wrecks document how treacherous to human judgment and equipment the deep cold and dark can be. Beyond that huge similarity, these two rail disasters illustrate significant differences in safety, transportation, culture, values, and even the response to disaster that nine decades can bring.

On Wednesday, February 14, 1900, NP freight #54 left Missoula at midday with thirty-nine cars of shingles, lumber, general merchandise, and a car of "giant powder." Missoula and Helena recorded -20° F. to -30° F. temperatures that day. The University in Missoula deemed it unwise to hold classes in such "rigorous" weather. Engineer Nelson Bostwick described cordwood fires in the roundhouse to keep thawed the oil for engine turntables. He said that, as they left town, "a new skim of snow was like sand and the drivers howled when I started for the main line." The train reached Blossburg, just west of Mullan Pass and before the Mullan Tunnel, slowly but without incident, and stopped.

By then, Bostwick had noticed that the train's airbrake system was not holding adequate pressure. He assumed that the "cold-stiffened air hoses were working their couplings, making a lot of small leaks." A week after the accident, Bostwick told Lewis and Clark County Coroner Dr. Ben C. Brooke that he had informed his two brakemen of the leaking hoses—a common cold-weather rail danger—and asked them to set handbrakes before and during the train's descent.

Forty years later, in an account for *Railroading Magazine*, Bostwick also said that he had telegraphed his superintendent for permission to bring the train into Helena in two segments. When the superintendent ridiculed him for excessive caution, Bostwick described himself as so mad that—rather than using his better judgment or seeking a third opinion—he stomped back to the train and highballed off the siding. He planned, he said, to divert disaster by "bunching" the train (keeping the cars close together) to reduce hose leakage, by stopping periodically to let the air pressure pump the line, and by counting on the brakemen to set handbrakes as needed.

Once underway through the Mullan Tunnel, the gauges seemed to indicate that bunching had increased the air-system pressure. But when Bostwick pulled the brake lever to slow down, nothing happened. Just after midnight on February 15, the steam engines howled through Iron Ridge Tunnel, derailed on the curve just outside, and plummeted into the gully below. Thirty-nine cars were "crushed into pieces like matchwood" within the fourteen-car-length tunnel.

Engineer Bostwick, Fireman L.G. Snider, and Brakeman Louis Schraeder jumped or were thrown clear to relative safety—though all suffered cuts and bruises. They were taken to Helena's St. Peter's Hospital and treated by Dr. George King. The NP's own doctor, William Treacy, was in Washington, D.C., to testify in Montana Senator William A. Clark's election-fraud hearings. The body of the second brakeman, J.L. Hinemayer, was found two days later. He had last been seen running along the top of the cars to set the brakes.

A week after the accident, the wreckage had been cleared—at the additional cost of the life of a Japanese rail-cleanup worker—and train service returned to that line. Coroner Brooke had completed his investigations into the death of Brakeman Hinemayer. That investigation revealed contradictory testimony between Engineer Bostwick, who blamed the brakemen for failing to set handbrakes, and Brakeman Schraeder, who saw no serious problems in the airhose system and said that he had not been told to set brakes at Blossburg. The newspapers described Bostwick as a fourteen-year NP veteran and Schraeder as an NP newcomer, with only a year's experience as a brakeman. Beyond that week, the newspaper carried no further coverage of the wreck, subsequent investigations, or changes in NP personnel or safety.

Throughout the week, as context for the accident, newspapers did note how many expensive pileups had occurred around the Iron Ridge Tunnel, with little loss of human life, and how rail equipment still needed much improvement. In his magazine article forty years later, Bostwick explained that, in his judgment, the final loss of air pressure occurred when a ball of ice formed within a coupling and blocked all air movement through the line.

Eighty-nine years later, Montana Rail Link #121 pulled out of the Laurel rail yards early Wednesday morning, February 1. It consisted of three diesel-powered locomotives and forty-nine cars. Sixteen additional cars had been removed because a first airbrake test noted failure "due to cold." Train #121 carried a radio telemetry end-of-train (EOT) device, but no caboose. Thirteen cars were empty; the remaining thirty-six carried plastics, corn, beer, soybeans, clays, syrup, cottonseed, and chemicals. The train reached Townsend at 6:00 P.M., after almost twice the ordinary running time. At Townsend, because they would exceed federal hours-of-service operating limits, the Laurel crew was replaced. The train left Townsend for Helena a little before midnight and experienced a range of delays due to the cold, including fluctuations in airbrake pressure.

Train #121 arrived in Helena at 3:10 A.M. on February 2. It left ten minutes later, with a new crew. At its very front, three additional MRL locomotives had been attached to help it across the Continental Divide. Those helper locomotives led the train out of town and up the grade. The road locomotives followed immediately behind the helper engines; the forty-nine cars came last. The temperature stood at -27° F., with wind a chill of -70° F. The road crew included an engineer, an assistant engineer, and a utility-operating employee. Another engineer

The 1989 wreck by daylight on February 2. View is west toward the hills through which the train rolled.

GENE FISCHER PHOTO/HELENA INDEPENDENT RECORD

and utility-operating employee manned the helper locomotives.

As the train climbed the Continental Divide—over trackage rebuilt to eliminate the curves and tunnels that had plagued the line eighty-nine years earlier—the lead locomotive in the helper unit lost heat and power. The crew also learned from the rail dispatcher that the cold was causing problems with the automatic signal-and-switching system. They would need to hand-operate the switches at the Austin sidings, thirteen miles out of Helena. Since the train had to stop anyway to accomplish this switching, the engineer in the defective helper engine told the dispatcher that he planned to exchange the helper locomotives for the road units. This exchange would put a functioning, warm engine on the front.

The National Transportation Safety Board's (NTSB) subsequent investigation shows that the road engineer for Train #121 argued with the helper engineer about the need to switch units. In fact, he offered to run the full train himself in the cold locomotive. The helper engineer refused the offer and stuck with his intention to switch locomotive sets. The road engineer did not argue further.

At 4:00 A.M., as the train stopped in West Austin, the road engineer found his instruments recording adequate airbrake pressure throughout the train. So, the crews went about the process of uncoupling and moving the helper locomotives away from the road engines, onto a siding. They then began to separate the road locomotives from the train to place them on the siding ahead of the helper locomotives. Next they made adjustments to the air-system valves (the angle cocks) to keep the train set.

Just before the road locomotives were separated from the train, the road engineer noticed a sharp decrease in airbrake pressure. His crewman then closed the angle cocks both on the last road locomotive and on the first car of the train, before uncoupling the train from the road locomotives. That represented a common cold-weather practice—used in lieu of putting the train's brakes into "emergency." Activating the airbrake emergency system tended to freeze controls at the end of train.

The crew chose not to set handbrakes for any of the cars—

despite requirements for doing so on mountain grades. In making that choice, they later described their sense that the switching time would be so short as to make it unnecessary and that "bottling"—partial rather than real emergency braking—was employed with some frequency.

As every resident of Helena that morning knows, the air-brake system did not hold the uncoupled cars. The cars careened down the grade toward a helper set of locomotives, stationed near the Benton Avenue crossing, that was preparing to boost another train over to Blossburg. When the crews at Austin realized, in the foggy, crystallized air, that the train had disappeared, they hurriedly connected the locomotives, tried to catch the runaway cars, and finally called the dispatcher to inform him of the runaway.

The two-person crew of the helper units at Benton Avenue may or may not have had any warning. The desperate call from Austin was transmitted on another channel, and the Benton Avenue men had been in and out of their engines just before the runaway cars hit. Miraculously unhurt, the helper crew at Benton radioed in the crash at 4:30 A.M. and then walked toward Benton Avenue beside the train. By the time a MRL yardmaster had reached the site, liquids from derailed cars were flowing along the track, licking into small fires in the debris. At 4:48 A.M., two enormous explosions at the site spewed wreckage around the vicinity, knocked out Helena's power, shattered nearby windows, and twisted and cracked buildings at the adjacent Elk River Cement Plant and at Carroll College.

By 5:30 A.M., city officials ordered the evacuation of a sixteen-block area. Train and emergency officials began combing MRL train manifest records to find out what chemicals had exploded and were still burning (acetone, isopropyl alcohol, and hydrogen peroxide). Within the day, local and state officials, MRL supervisors, and NTSB staff began the painstaking process of figuring out why the accident had occurred, what damages it had caused (finally estimated at more than $6 million), and what changes they needed to institute in rail operations and emergency procedures. On December 6, 1989, ten months later, the NTSB published its findings:

The probable cause of this accident was the fail-

*ure of the crew of train 1-121-28 to properly secure
their train by placing the train brakes in emergency
and applying hand brakes when it was left standing
unattended on a mountain grade. Contributing to the
accident was the decision of the engineer of Helper 2
to rearrange the locomotive consist [configuration]
and leave the train unattended on the mountain grade,
and the effects of the extreme cold weather on the airbrake system of the train and its crewmembers....*

Between these two February runaway-train wrecks, what
are the important similarities and the important differences?
In context, impact, and reaction, the two accidents are entirely different. In 1900, train wrecks and train injuries were common. In anticipation of this reality, the NP placed its own doctor and its own hospital in Missoula. For all long-distance
transportation, trains were the only way that people and goods
traveled.

As Montanans now take highway accidents for granted,
Montanans in 1900 assumed a certain risk to all train activity.
Helena trainmen actually found the Iron Mountain Tunnel so
daunting as to predict their own deaths there. Further, in 1900,
however intriguing and correctable the cause of that wreck
might have been, no public agencies investigated the tragedy.
The National Transportation Safety Board was not established
until 1967, the successor to several generations of less-inten-
sive safety and regulatory federal programs.

Safety considerations, in general, had changed rail operation substantially by 1989. Federal requirements to limit the
hours that a crew worked accounted for a series of MRL #121
train delays. In 1900, Engineer Bostwick explained that he
made the Missoula-to-Helena run fifteen to eighteen times a
month, working hours far beyond those permitted a 1989 crew.

When MRL #121 left Laurel, it was subjected to both a "roll-
by" inspection and to an airbrake-system inspection. In 1900,
the crew used no formal procedures to check equipment. In
1989, Train #121 was equipped with an event recorder, similar to an airplane's "black box," that offered investigators a
way to corroborate testimony.

By 1989 in Montana, train crews relied on end-of-train devices rather than on personal communication between cabooses and locomotives. The NTSB concluded that the transmission from the EOT on MRL #121 was blocked by the mountainous terrain around Austin and did not reach its locomotives—a point quickly noted by several Montana legislators who had opposed eliminating cabooses in an earlier session.

The most important similarity between the two crashes was the February cold. In both cases, brutal temperatures took a major toll on how equipment and people functioned. Train personnel from both eras found that the cold ate up precious time and energy, made them reluctant to work outside any longer than necessary, and forced them to guess at what might be plaguing their equipment. The NTSB report notes that the temperature on January 31, 1989, had been +25° F. and then had dropped to -27° F. by February 2. That explained why one employee had reached his shift wearing uninsulated cowboy boots and sought a way to handle the brakes without walking the train's length.

In both crashes, trainmen said that cold temperatures were commonplace and that new equipment was supposed to function in severe cold. But just the same, in subtle and sometimes untraceable ways, the equipment (steam-powered in 1900 and diesel-driven in 1989) did not work predictably. Solutions for braking that might have worked even at zero did not work in 1900, nor ninety years later—despite considerable modernization and safety precautions—when temperatures fell still lower.

Perhaps the second most intriguing similarity between these crashes is quirky human interaction and choice. In the 1900 NP wreck, engineer Bostwick blamed the brakemen for failing to set the brakes and blamed his superintendent for ridiculing his fears. He acknowledged, ultimately, that he could have waited for additional advice.

In 1989, the two engineers on Train #121 did not know who legally was in charge—the helper-locomotive engineer or the road engineer. It was the road engineer who disagreed with the need to switch engines. Yet, by his own account, he did not choose to argue the point further with his peer. As a 1900 newspaper put it, "not the best of feeling" existed on either crew. Critical cold then exacerbated those working relations.

In both accidents, the length of rail-employee service and the adequacy of knowledge and training were at issue in subsequent investigations. And, in both accidents, decisions on how to handle the train ping-ponged between rules and "common practice"—with common practice deemed at fault in both instances.

The cost of such events is intolerable—no matter what the era. The 1989 crash and explosion, which occurred within Helena proper, triggered fear and huge property damage. Like all communities of its size, Helena had a disaster-emergency preparedness plan and put that into effect—complete with command posts. Carroll College students received an unanticipated holiday until basic repairs could be made.

But the stress of the event left nearby residents waking up at 5:00 A.M. for mornings thereafter, anticipating another explosion. And in 1900, however casually the newspapers treated it, however fatalistic trainmen were about accidents, two people died.

There is a reason why Helenans welcome any sign of spring on dark and cold February nights.

WERE GERMANS READY TO INVADE THE MONTANA CAPITAL?

BY MARTHA KOHL

On September 1, 1917, the front page of the Helena *Independent* read:

AIRPLANE SEEN FLYING ABOVE HELENA
HAVE GERMANS SPY POST NEAR HERE?

The United States had entered World War I the previous April, joining Britain in the fight against Germany. Until Armistice Day, November 1918, thoughts of war consumed Montanans.

Rumors of a German invasion of Helena continued to build throughout the fall of 1917, with frequent reports in the *Independent* fanning its readers' fears. A front-page story in October asked: "Are the Germans about to bomb the capital of Montana? Have they spies in the Mountain fastnesses equipped with wireless stations and aeroplanes? Do our enemies fly around over our high mountains where formerly only the shadow of the eagle swept?"

On the first of November, citizens infuriated by the mysterious airplane's repeated visits reportedly "emptied a high-power rapid-fire gun at the raider." They failed to down the plane. Governor Sam Stewart pledged his assistance: "Notify me at once next time," he was quoted as saying, "and I will pursue in my auto. This thing must be run down." No one actually saw a plane—just mysterious blinking lights. Nor did reporters stop to ask why the Germans would want to bomb Helena. War hysteria had overtaken the city—and, especially, the offices of the *Helena Independent*.

When President Woodrow Wilson ordered troops to France, he also unleashed a massive propaganda effort to rally the

Second Montana, 163rd Infantry, leaving for France on October 24, 1917, received a downtown Helena send-off.

American people to the war. "It is not an army we must shape and train for war, it is a nation," he declared. Newspaper editors across the country responded. The result, in Helena as elsewhere, was the fostering of "super patriotism."

The Helena Home Guard, which drilled regularly, formed an espionage branch to investigate suspicious characters, suspected spies, and disloyal people. News media in Helena and across the country urged "wheatless days" and "meatless days" to assure enough food for the army, and an editorial in the *Helena Independent* proposed that high school students wear khaki uniforms with insignia to cut down on clothing needs and as a constant reminder that the country was at war.

All things German became suspect—even the German language. Across the nation, "hamburgers" became "liberty sandwiches," while "sauerkraut" became "liberty cabbage." In Helena, the *Independent* attacked Montana's only German language newspaper, the Helena *Staats-Zeitung*, questioning not only the paper's loyalty, but also the loyalty of its advertisers.

All "alien enemies"—citizens of the German empire living in the United States—had to register with the U.S. government. In Helena, they registered at the police station, where their photographs and fingerprints were taken. The Helena School Board banned the teaching of German in April 1918. A statewide ban on the use of German in the classroom and from the pulpit soon reenforced its decision. The ban was issued by the Montana Council of Defense, a board appointed by Governor Stewart and vested by the legislature with the power to promulgate orders "which are necessary or proper for the public safety and for the protection of life and public property."

The council followed up its language ban by hiring Helena lawyer John G. Brown to read books about Germany in school libraries to make sure that they did not contain pro-German propaganda. Brown had earlier written the council expressing his outrage that forty-two Montana high schools assigned a history textbook that claimed Germans had made great contributions to western civilization.

The purchase of Liberty bonds to help fund the war became a measure of patriotism. In Helena, women went door-to-door selling Liberty bonds, and Lewis and Clark County bond drives consistently raised more than their targets. Ostensibly, subscribing to the Liberty bond campaign was voluntary, but those who refused to purchase bonds—or who did not purchase bonds in large-enough quantities—were harassed and ostracized.

Of course, German-Americans who failed to subscribe were particularly suspect. The Lewis and Clark County Liberty bond campaign went so far as to take out a three-column advertisement in the *Independent* denouncing Reinholdt Kleinschmidt for refusing to buy bonds.

Born in Prussia, Kleinschmidt was one of the most prominent merchants in the state. The *Independent*'s editor was William Campbell, an influential member of both the Montana Council of Defense and the Lewis and Clark County Liberty bond committee. He editorialized: "The spirit of some people with regard to buying Liberty bonds is contemptible, disloyal and bordering on treason."

Not only German-Americans suffered from the zealous prosecution of the war at home. Ironically, the war the U.S. entered to "make the world safe for democracy" served at home to suppress dissent, stifle free speech, and foster intolerance.

The general view was reflected in a *Helena Independent* editorial shortly after the U.S. declared war: "internal dissension must disappear when we are threatened with grave danger from without." Or, as the *Independent* more bluntly put it in another editorial: "Shut up or be locked up."

The targets of these *Helena Independent* articles were the socialists and members of the labor organization Industrial Workers of the World (IWW), who condemned the war as "a capitalist plot," as well as Irish nationalists who opposed any alliance with England. Butte and the western Montana lumber camps were IWW strongholds, and many from among Butte's large Irish-American population supported Irish independence.

Much to the frustration of the editor of the *Helena Independent* and other "super patriots," criticizing the war was protected at first as free speech. That changed when Governor Stewart called a special legislative session, and the Montana Legislature passed the Montana Sedition Act on February 3, 1918. The act made it illegal during wartime to criticize the armed forces, the constitution, or the state or federal government.

The Montana Sedition Act became the model for the Federal Sedition Act, one of the most sweeping violations of civil liberties in modern American history. This outlawing of free speech—passed under the guise of wartime emergency—was primarily a political weapon directed against the radical farmer and labor organizations fighting to improve the conditions of farmers, agricultural laborers, loggers, and miners.

In fact, however, anyone caught speaking against the war could, and often was, prosecuted. Burton Wheeler, then serving as Montana's attorney general, later remembered that feuding neighbors provided most of the "tips" his office received on violations of the Sedition Act.

The most famous trial for sedition held in Helena was that of William Dunn, the editor of the socialist *Butte Bulletin*. Dunn was a communist, a fervent unionist, and a longtime critic of the Anaconda Company. He was arrested for sedition on a Lewis and Clark County warrant for writing editorials criticizing the Montana Council of Defense.

That his editorials did not circulate in Helena was immaterial to those who orchestrated his arrest. They wanted Dunn's trial held in Helena because they feared that no Butte jury would convict him. The Helena jury did convict, but their decision was overturned by the Montana Supreme Court, which found that no crime had been committed.

Dunn's trial was just one example of political persecution during the war. World War I provided a reason—or an excuse—to suppress free speech and move against dissenters like Dunn, who were accused of "serving the Kaiser." In fact, the *Helena Independent* and other conservative newspapers consistently branded any labor agitation as "pro-German."

Prosecution of dissenters did not end on Armistice Day; raids against the IWW and arrests and deportations conducted in the name of public safety continued into the 1920s during what has become known as America's first Red Scare. Intolerance and the denial of civil liberties, unleashed in a fit of war hysteria, proved hard to reign in again.

THE NORWEGIAN
SPECIAL, 1939

꧁꧂

BY DAVE WALTER

Before World War II, when transcontinental railroads thrived, Helena served as a major destination for national and international dignitaries. After all, it was Montana's capital city. And more than fifteen Northern Pacific and Great Northern trains daily served the community.

Presidents Teddy Roosevelt (1903), Howard Taft (1909), Franklin D. Roosevelt (1920), and Harry S. Truman (1948) customarily stopped in Helena. Such entertainers as Sarah Bernhardt (1891), Mark Twain (1895), Ignace Paderewski (1900), Ethel Barrymore (1927), and Dinah Shore (1949) also made Helena a regular stop. Even an occasional member of European royalty—for instance, Queen Marie of Rumania (1928)—chose Helena for her sole Montana appearance.

By the 1950s, however, the pattern had shifted. With a growing reliance on airplane travel, Helena began to decline as a logical destination. Planes allowed dignitaries to move about quickly and to select larger Montana cities—for instance, Butte, and Great Falls, and Missoula. More and more frequently, Helena's small population eliminated it from the travel schedules of the great and the near-great.

One of the last gala events typical of the railroad era occurred on May 29, 1939. On the eve of World War II, Helena hosted their royal highnesses Crown Prince Olav and his wife, Crown Princess Martha. These representatives of Norway's hereditary constitutional monarchy stopped here for a single-day visit. On this occasion, the Capital City produced a whirlwind series of events worthy of visiting royalty.

In the spring of 1939, Adolf Hitler's German forces were just months from sweeping through Poland and the Low Countries. Within a year, Norway itself would be invaded. In April

1939, however, the Crown Prince and Princess had journeyed to New York City, to open the Norwegian pavilion at the 1939 World's Fair at Flushing Meadows. They then embarked on a ten-week goodwill tour of the United States that would take them from the East Coast to the Pacific Ocean and back again. By the end of May, they were returning east from California— most recently having left Hollywood, San Francisco, Portland and Spokane.

The invitation to visit Helena had been extended by Montana Governor Roy E. Ayers and by the 1939 Montana Legislature, via Senate Joint Resolution #6. The city had delegated arrangements to a Helena Chamber of Commerce committee headed by Trevor O. Hammond, the president of the First National Bank and Trust Company. For weeks prior to the occasion, Hammond had worked feverishly. He confidently promised "one of the greatest holidays in Helena's history."

The chamber predicted that between 2,000 and 3,000 Montanans (most of them of Scandinavian descent) would inundate Helena to see "one of the most distinguished parties ever to visit Montana." The cost of the celebration fell neither on the state, nor on the city, nor on the chamber. Private contributions from Norman B. Holter, the First National Bank and Trust Company, the Union Bank and Trust Company, Fligelman's Department Store, and the Montana Power Company covered all expenses.

The Prince and Princess and their entourage would arrive in Helena at 10:35 A.M. and depart at 6:15 P.M. So T.O. Hammond created a tight schedule that featured the Vigilante Day parade at 12:00 noon, a luncheon for more than 1,000 people at the Civic Center ballroom at 2:00, an audience with Helena children in the Center auditorium at 3:15, and an automobile excursion into the Helena Valley to inspect the Porter Brothers' gold dredge.

To honor the royal visit, Governor Ayers proclaimed May 29 a legal holiday in Montana and designated it "Velkommen [Welcome] Day." The Governor remarked that, since so many Norwegians had settled Montana, it was only fitting to close state, county, and city offices for the full day on Monday. Hammond noted in a speech to the Exchange Club (Helena *Mon-*

Norway's Crown Prince Olav and Crown Princess Martha, in Glacier National Park shortly after being given these outfits and tack at a banquet in Helena on May 29, 1939.

tana Record-Herald, May 27, 1939):

> *Behind this reception is a tremendous feeling of goodwill on the part of Montana for Norway, particularly because of her position in an increasingly hostile world. This feeling will be lavished on the royal couple because they are Norway's official representatives. All indications are that Helena's crowd Monday will be one of the largest in the history of the city.*

At 8:30 on the morning of May 29, a Helena delegation boarded "the Norwegian special" train at Garrison and rode with the Prince and Princess over Mullan Pass to Helena. The group comprised Mr. and Mrs. Hammond, Matt Staff (the Chamber of Commerce's secretary-manager) and his wife, and attorney Edmund G. Toomey (in charge of introductions at the Northern Pacific depot) and his wife. The Norwegian party numbered 13, including official press representatives, photographers, and four personal servants. Prince Olav and Princess Martha—both in their late thirties—were not accompanied to North America by their three children, Princesses Ragnhild and Astrid, and two-year-old Prince Harald. (The same Harald V is the current king of Norway.)

At least an hour before "the Norwegian special" arrived at the Northern Pacific depot, crowds began to gather in Beattie Park and along Helena Avenue. Promptly at 10:35, the smiling, waving dignitaries stepped from the train, to be greeted by Governor Ayers and Helena Mayor Albert J. Roberts. Prince Olav appeared in a dark business suit. Princess Martha was attired in "a blue and white French-print dress and carried a cape of silver fox fur. She sported a black taffeta beret-affect hat and diamond eardrops. She wore this outfit throughout the day (*Helena Independent*, May 30, 1939)."

Five-year-old Marilyn Hovde, the daughter of Oscar and Elva Hovde, presented Princess Martha with a beautiful bouquet of flowers donated by the State Nursery and Seed Company. Other women in the party received corsages from the Knox Flower Shop.

In a very emotional moment, the Prince and Princess were welcomed to Helena by Miss Pauline Holter, the granddaughter of pioneer Helena capitalist Anton M. Holter (1831-1921). In 1918, Norway's King Haakon VII had made Holter a knight of the first class, Order of St. Olav, "for distinguished service to his native country in a time of crisis." In many ways, Holter epitomized the Norwegian immigrant who had built Montana commerce and society.

Security for the royal visit fell to a phalanx of Montana highway patrolmen mounted on motorcycles, uniformed city and county police, and a contingent from the Montana National Guard. Led by the motorcycle escort, the procession moved up Helena Avenue to the Placer Hotel (on the south side of Grand Street, between Main and Jackson). Waves of applause cascaded over the lead automobile. In addition to the touring cars for dignitaries, two Yellowstone Park Company open busses carried the rest of the party. Many homes flew American and Scandinavian flags from their porches, and most business blocks decorated with bunting and flags.

The entire seventh floor of the Placer Hotel had been reserved for the Norwegian delegation. Here the couple rested briefly before holding a press conference, at which they lavished praise on Helenans for their hospitality.

Precisely at 11:30, the official party returned to its motorcade. This time the escort mixed motorcycle patrolmen with a band of mounted cowboys from Lincoln. The cars slowly drove through town—again to constant cheers and shouts—to the reviewing stand in Women's Park. Normally the bandstand, this structure had been decorated elaborately with bunting, pine boughs, and grizzly-bear hides. While awaiting the Vigilante Day parade, Helena High School students executed a flag demonstration, performed several folk dances, and sang patriotic songs in front of the dignitaries.

Helena officials had rescheduled the Sixteenth Annual Vigilante Day parade for the royal visit and billed it as "an hourlong history lesson" for Olav and Martha. The *Independent* editorialized (May 28, 1939):

> *From the Vigilante Parade the princely visitors will be able to derive, in an enjoyable hour, a better idea of the history and the development of the Great Northwest than by any other method of enlightenment imaginable. The Vigilante Parade is educational. Its depictions are as accurate as varied. They cause the thrilling Montana past to rise before the eye as no other instruction could.*

The students interspersed the usual scenes of pioneer Montana with special floats that honored Scandinavian contributions to the state. The Prince and Princess applauded each entry and spontaneously stood to snap photos of many floats as they passed the reviewing stand. Organizers justly concluded that the parade was the longest and the most elaborate ever held. Helena police estimated that more than 14,000 persons viewed the procession under sunny skies.

Immediately following the parade, Governor Ayers introduced the Crown Prince and the Crown Princess to the crowd assembled in Women's and Hill parks. Prince Olav's remarks—delivered in both English and Norwegian—focused on the rapid commercial growth of the American West. He said (*Record-Herald*, May 29, 1939):

> *We have been proud, here and everywhere on our trip, for the praise given the Norwegian people who came early to your West and helped develop it. We have been proud of the fine positions they have made for*

themselves in the communities of your country where they have settled, particularly in Montana.

The motorcade then whisked the dignitaries up the hill to the Civic Center ballroom for an official luncheon and reception. Although the meal was scheduled for 2:00, almost 1,000 guests had taken their places at the ballroom tables well in advance. Hundreds more paid fifty cents each to stand and view the event from the balcony. The royal table was lavishly set with crystal and silver and beautifully decorated with red geraniums and mignonette. The *Independent* enthused:

The stage in the ballroom has been decorated, in typical Western fashion, with evergreens and mountain flowers, and a life-size model of a brown horse stands in the trees. On the model has been fitted some of the gifts for the royal visitors—a silver-inlaid saddle and bridle. Their chaps and other pieces of riding equipment have been mounted on each side of the horse. The two riding outfits were manufactured in Miles City.

When the royal party entered, a long ovation ensued. Ushers and waitresses clad in Norwegian costumes served the meal. Meanwhile, Louise Wood Tompkins played two piano solos, "Dance of the Dwarfs" and "To Spring," by Norwegian composer Edvard Grieg, and then accompanied Octavia Rider Young who performed two violin solos, "Chalet Girl's Sunday," by Ole Bull, and "Solveig's Song," from the *Peer Gynt Suite* by Grieg. Both the crowd and the dignitaries applauded the performances enthusiastically.

After a series of formal introductions, Prince Olav delivered a short address in English. Helena radio station KPFA carried his remarks live for those Helenans who had not purchased tickets to the event. Then the Prince and Princess excused themselves from the ballroom and entered the Civic Center auditorium. Here a crowd of hundreds of Helena school children had gathered to greet the royal couple and to sing the Norwegian national anthem—in Norwegian. A girls' drill team from the American Legion auxiliary also performed a spirited routine that brought applause and praise from the Princess.

Upon returning to the ballroom, Olav and Martha received

elaborate gifts from "the Norwegian people of Montana." Purchased with statewide contributions totalling more than $1,500, the presents were delivered by Montana State College student Miss Ruth Undem from Terry. The Prince and the Princess sportingly donned large, white cowboy hats to accept the two complete Western riding outfits. In addition, the Prince received the Western saddle and bridle, detailed in silver. The couple would wear these gifts within a week, when they rode saddle horses in both Yellowstone and Glacier national parks.

The last event on the official schedule specifically had been requested by Prince Olav. He wanted to see how an electrified gold dredge operated. So the motorcade left the Civic Center at 4:00 and toured out to the Porter Brothers' location north of Custer Avenue. For forty-five minutes, both the Prince and Princess climbed all over the dredge, asking myriad questions of superintendent Bill Wells. Security officers and photographers could not keep up with the pair, so waited on deck during their excursion. True to organizer Hammond's schedule, the entourage motored back to the Placer Hotel at 5:00 and rested briefly.

Promptly at 5:45, the royal party returned to their automobiles and followed the motorcycle escort back to the Northern Pacific depot. Again crowds lined the streets to catch a last glimpse of the couple and to cheer them wildly. At the depot, the Prince formally thanked his hosts and remarked on Helena's overwhelming hospitality (*Record-Herald*, May 31, 1939):

> *I am sure the parade will remain with us as one of the pleasantest experiences we have had on our entire trip. To be able to visualize the building and development of Montana in this way has been wonderful.*
>
> *One thing that has impressed us especially in Helena is the easy, extemporaneous way in which the speeches of welcome and presentation have been made. In other places, such speeches are often written out and read with much nervousness. Here a spontaneous spirit of friendliness and good fellowship has prevailed. The words of welcome and compliment have been so sincere and unaffected that they made a deep impression on us.*

One event that the royal couple could not share was a dance and reception held on Monday evening in the Civic Center ballroom. Sponsored by the Scandinavian Fraternity, it would conclude events for both Helenans and out-of-town Scandinavian visitors. Admittance was free to all holders of luncheon tickets, and the gala ran well beyond midnight.

The final touch to this remarkable visit by Crown Prince Olav and Crown Princess Martha occurred as "the Norwegian special" slowly pulled away from the Northern Pacific depot, on its way to Livingston and Yellowstone National Park. As Olav and Martha stood on the rear platform of their private car, a man from the crowd shouted, "Good-bye, Ole." The Crown Prince grasped the democratic spirit of the farewell, caught the man's eye, waved at him, and smiled broadly.

As "the Norwegian special" steamed into the May evening, the people of Helena also were saying good-bye to an era of special visits to the Capital City, based on the transcontinental railroad system. Fittingly, they had feted the Norwegian couple in grand style.

INDEX

Italic numerals indicate illustrations

Jon Axline, a Montana native, can trace his roots in Helena, through the Adami Family, back to 1872. As a Cultural Resource Specialist/Historian for the Montana Department of Transportation, he has had the opportunity to visit many of the places, famous, infamous and less well known, where Montana's history was made.

Ellen Baumler, a Kansas native, taught for ten years in Tucson, Arizona, before moving to Helena in 1988. With a Ph.D. in medieval studies and three summers of co-directing a field school in Italy, she now takes delight in the accessibility and relevance of Helena's history. Ellen coordinates Montana's National Register of Historic Places sign program at the State Historic Preservation Office.

David Cole, a former resident of East Helena, is Chief of the Community Development Bureau of the Montana Department of Commerce. The bureau administers federal- and state-funded programs that assist communities in financing public-facility projects, including adequate water systems to provide fire protection.

Chere Jiusto is a historian and ceramic artist who has lived in Helena for many years.

Martha Kohl is the editor of the Montana Historical Society Press.

Leanne Kurtz is a Helena native currently employed as a researcher with the Montana Legislative Services Division.

Harriett C. Meloy came to Helena in the early 1930s. She is active in many local and state organizations. She was on the staff of the Montana Historical Society library from 1957 to 1977. She also served on the original board of the Lewis and Clark County Historical Society.

Vivian A. Paladin, a native of Glasgow, has lived in Helena since 1956. A newspaper typesetter, reporter and editor since high school days, she was asked by K. Ross Toole to join the editorial staff of Montana: The Magazine of Western History in 1958. As associate editor and then for a dozen years editor, she saw the journal become a publication notable for solid historical content and a high degree of pleasing design and readability.

Sara Scott is an archaeologist who first came to Helena in 1979. She holds a Master's degree in Anthropology from the University of Oregon and has been doing archaeological field work and research since 1976. She recently wrote, with a Helena teacher, an archaeology curriculum program for Montana public school children in grades three through eight. Her research on prehistoric shelter and stone tool production and quarrying appears in several regional archaeology journals.

Dave Shors is Associate Editor of the Helena *Independent Record*.

Stephenie Ambrose Tubbs does historical research for Ambrose Tubbs Inc., and resides in Helena year-round.

Dave Walter has been employed by the Montana Historical Society for eighteen years and currently is the Society's research historian.

Marcella Walter currently works for the Parks Division, Montana Department of Fish, Wildlife and Parks, encouraging the preservation and interpretation of Montana's splendid historic, natural, and recreational resources. She's a Kansan transplanted to Montana by way of a ten-year National Park Service career in Gettysburg, Pennsylvania, and Washington, D.C. Prior to working for State Parks, she was Montana's State Historic Preservation Officer and the Montana Historical Society's Education Officer.